Is Your Church Ready?

Also by Ravi Zacharias and Norman Geisler

Who Made God? And Answers to Over 100 Other Tough Questions of Faith

IS YOUR CHURCH READY?

MOTIVATING LEADERS TO LIVE AN APOLOGETIC LIFE

RAVI ZACHARIAS
NORMAN GEISLER
GENERAL EDITORS

GRAND RAPIDS, MICHIGAN 49530 USA

ZONDERVAN™

Is Your Church Ready?
Copyright © 2003 by Ravi Zacharias and Norman Geisler

Requests for information should be addressed to:
Zondervan, *Grand Rapids, Michigan 49530*

Library of Congress Cataloging-in-Publication Data

Is your church ready? : motivating leaders to live an apologetic life / Ravi Zacharias
and Norman Geisler, general editors.
    p. cm.
    Includes bibliographical references (p. 159) and indexes.
    ISBN 0-310-25061-7
    1. Apologetics. 2. Evangelistic work. I. Zacharias, Ravi K. II. Geisler, Norman L.
BT1103.I8 2003
239—dc21

    2003008392

This edition printed on acid-free paper.

All Scripture quotations, unless otherwise indicated, are taken from the *Holy Bible: New International Version*®. NIV®. Copyright © 1973, 1978, 1984 by International Bible Society. Used by permission of Zondervan. All rights reserved.

Scripture quotations marked AMP NT are taken from the Amplified ® New Testament. Copyright © 1954, 1958, 1987 by the Lockman Foundation. Used by permission.

Scripture quotations marked AMP OT are taken from the Amplified Bible, Old Testament. Copyright © 1965, 1987 by Zondervan. Used by permission.

Scripture quotations marked KJV are taken from the King James Version of the Bible.

Scripture quotations marked RSV are taken from the *Revised Standard Version of the Bible*, copyright 1946, 1952, 1971 by the Division of Christian Education of the National Council of the Churches of Christ in the USA. Used by permission.

Published in association with the literary agency of Wolgemuth & Associates, Inc.

Interior design by Tracey Moran

Printed in the United States of America

---

03 04 05 06 07 08 09 /❖ DC/ 10 9 8 7 6 5 4 3 2 1

CONTENTS

Acknowledgments 7

Preface 9

Contributors 11

1. The Pastor as an Apologist 15
   RAVI ZACHARIAS

2. Four Challenges for Church Leaders 25
   RAVI ZACHARIAS

3. The Church as the Heart and Soul of Apologetics . . 39
   JOHN GUEST

4. The Priority of Apologetics in the Church 55
   PETER J. GRANT

5. Arrows and Swords in the Church 73
   RAVI ZACHARIAS

6. Creating an Apologetic Climate in the Home 89
JUDY SALISBURY

7. Off to College: Can We Keep Them? 103
J. BUDZISZEWSKI

8. Issues and Approaches in Working with Internationals . . 125
DEAN C. HALVERSON

Appendix: Church Leaders' Annotated Resource Guide . . 149

Notes 159

Scripture Index 167

Subject Index 169

Acknowledgments

M any have contributed to this effort. In the early days, Joan Cattell, research assistant to Norman Geisler, labored hard to get every contributor's work in place. Her patience was a good example of an apologist with a kindly disposition. Danielle DuRant, Ravi Zacharias's research assistant, served as managing editor and worked unselfishly and round the clock to bring it to the publisher in a well-organized and complete manuscript. Without her, we would never have met all the deadlines. Our sincere thanks go out to her. The many writers in these volumes and the valued assistance of Zondervan's editorial staff deserve our heartfelt thanks as well. We are grateful to God that the work finally hit the press.

Ravi K. Zacharias
Norman L. Geisler

PREFACE

The book you have in your hands is the fruit of the vision of Dr. Norman Geisler, who has labored long to equip church leaders—and others who desire to share the gospel winsomely and effectively—to be apologists. While Ravi Zacharias pays tribute to him in the accompanying volume titled *Who Made God?* in which his writings are highlighted, it is appropriate to acknowledge his contribution in soliciting authors and chapters for this book as well.

In John 13 we witness Jesus tenderly washing his disciples' feet, knowing that only hours later he would be betrayed by one and abandoned by the others on his way to the cross. Jesus says to them, "If I then, your Lord and Teacher, have *washed your feet,* you also ought to *wash one another's feet.* For I have given you an example, that you also should do as I have done to you" (verses 14–15 RSV, emphasis mine). This unique parallel construction of linking identical phrases such as "washed . . . feet" and "wash . . . feet" by using the word *ought* is found four times in the writings of John, who is identified as the disciple whom Jesus loved. For example, in 1 John 2:6, John writes that if we abide in Christ, we "ought to *walk* in the same way in which he *walked*" (RSV). And in 1 John 3:16 and 4:11, this same parallelism links *ought* with laying down one's life and loving others: Just as God has loved us sacrificially, so ought we to love. It seems particularly significant, then, that we first hear this phrase from Jesus immediately upon washing his disciples' feet, because Jesus is essentially *mirroring*—by both his words and his actions—what a servant-teacher is.

Jesus' model of the servant-teacher is a high calling to church leaders, but then again, it is a high calling to each of us as his disciples, whatever our principal calling may be. And it is with this understanding that this volume came to be. Thus, whereas the content is aimed in a certain measure to pastors and church leaders for the work of apologetics—that is, "to give an answer" *(apologia)* for the hope of the gospel within you (1 Peter 3:15 KJV)—the objective goes beyond that. Many of us are also parents or students or young professionals wrestling with questions that perplex not only the intellect but also the heart. With that in mind, we hope that you will ponder this: We are not only called to give answers but, as Ravi Zacharias writes, to be *answer bearers,* often to respond with gentle hands and swift feet rather than with words alone. This is the incarnational model Jesus demonstrates to us throughout the Gospels, and it is the example we hope you will find fleshed out in the chapters before you.

Danielle DuRant,
research assistant to Ravi Zacharias

CONTRIBUTORS

J. Budziszewski

J. Budziszewski (Ph.D., Yale, 1981), a nationally known scholar of natural law, holds joint appointments in the departments of Government and Philosophy at the University of Texas at Austin. He is the author of six scholarly books, most recently *What We Can't Not Know: A Guide* (Spence Publishing, 2002), as well as a book of apologetics titled *How to Stay Christian in College* (NavPress, 1999). Dr. Budziszewski also composes a monthly column, "Office Hours," for *Boundless,* an Internet magazine for Christian college students (http://www.boundless.org). He has contributed numerous articles to both academic and Christian journals. His current research focuses on the personal and cultural pathologies that flow from the repression of moral knowledge—from trying to convince ourselves that we don't know what we really do know about right and wrong.

Peter J. Grant

The Reverend Dr. Peter J. Grant is senior pastor of Cumberland Community Church in the suburbs of Atlanta, Georgia, where he has served since its inception. The church has established a pioneering ministry in apologetics, "Reasons for Faith," to equip believers and to engage with the culture in articulating a Christian worldview. The church also has a close affiliation with several apologetics ministries in the Atlanta area, and Dr. Grant has served on the board of the Faith and Science Lecture Forum, a ministry that has sponsored debates between leading scientists and philosophers and Christian apologists such as Dr. William Lane Craig, Dr. Ravi Zacharias, and Dr. Norman Geisler.

John Guest

John Guest was born and raised in Oxford, England, and came to Christ after hearing Billy Graham at a crusade in London. He himself has now spoken to more than 1.5 million people face to face since his first major crusade in 1985. He has been called "the thinking person's evangelist," a term that rightly describes his gift for combining brilliant apologetics with a powerful speaking style that has earned the respect of historical critics of crusade evangelism. John Guest graduated from Trinity College in Bristol and came to the United States in 1964, where he formed one of the first Christian contemporary music groups, the Excursions, drawing thousands of young people to meetings to hear the gospel. He is founder of the Coalition of Christian Outreach, a unique evangelistic organization employing approximately 150 staff workers on college campuses. He also cofounded Trinity Episcopal School of Ministry and was a participant in the Lausanne Committee on World Evangelism and a board member of the National Association of Evangelicals. The author of ten books, John Guest is presently pastor of Christ Church at Grove Farm in Sewickley, Pennsylvania.

Dean C. Halverson

Dean Halverson has been working with International Students, Inc., since 1988. He serves as the director of apologetics and as campus minister. During his years with ISI he has had the joy of getting to know numerous international students from all over the world and of sharing the love of Christ with them. He has authored *Crystal Clear* (NavPress, 1990), a discussion guide for witnessing to New Agers, and edited *The Compact Guide to World Religions* (Bethany House, 1996), which has been translated into Russian. Prior to his time with ISI, Dean Halverson worked as a researcher and writer with the Spiritual Counterfeits Project in Berkeley, California.

Judy Salisbury

Judy Salisbury is a wife and mother who speaks nationally on a wide variety of subjects from Christian apologetics to Christian living. Her speaking opportunities range from youth groups to women's retreats and large national conferences. As founder of Logos Presentations, Judy specializes in the area of equipping Christian leaders with effective communication and presentation skills through consultation, critique, and training. She is creator of the unique compact disc series *Divine Appointments: Spontaneous Conversations on Matters of the Heart, Soul, and Mind,* and author of the communication training manual *A Time to Speak* (foreword by Josh McDowell) and *A Christian Woman's Guide to Reasons for Faith,* a book on Christian apologetics written specifically for women.

Ravi Zacharias

Ravi Zacharias has spoken in countries worldwide and at numerous universities, notably Harvard, Cambridge, and Princeton. He received his Master of Divinity from Trinity Evangelical Divinity School and was a visiting scholar at Cambridge University. He has received three honorary doctorates. Dr. Zacharias is well versed in the disciplines of comparative religions, cults, and philosophy, and he held the chair of evangelism and contemporary thought at Alliance Theological Seminary for three and a half years. He has written several books, including *Jesus Among Other Gods, Cries of the Heart,* and *Can Man Live Without God?* He is heard weekly on the radio program *Let My People Think.* Dr. Zacharias is president of Ravi Zacharias International Ministries, headquartered in Atlanta, Georgia, with additional offices in Canada, India, Singapore, and the United Kingdom.

Chapter 1

THE PASTOR AS AN APOLOGIST

RAVI ZACHARIAS

A n old limerick says:
> There was a young student at Trinity,
> Who cracked the square root of infinity.
> But to work with the digits
> Gave him such fidgets
> He chucked math and took up divinity.

Whoever penned these words certainly communicated his or her prejudice successfully: that of all academic pursuits, the Christian ministry is the least engaging of the intellect. This is a most unfortunate caricature, but in a world given to stigmas, it is hard to shake. On a recent visit to France, as my wife and I were being escorted to the Bible college where I was to speak, the student driving us said, "Here in France, if I told my friends that my goal in life is to go to the moon, they would find it more credible than that I am a student at a Bible college." I listened with sadness. In the land of Pascal, Voltaire still sneers because nothing could be so "mindless" as one heading for a theological education.

Distortions are always discomforting, but we would do well to search for any fragment of truth in such sweeping castigations by critics of the Christian faith. To do so, however, we must ask ourselves some

hard questions. When I say hard, I do not mean questions that are stren-
uous to the mind as much as I mean questions that are tough on the
conscience. Has the communication of the most precious message of
all been diminished or deemed bereft of any intellectual credibility
because that is the way it really is, or because we have *made* it to be
that way? For communication to be effective, especially in matters as
life-defining as the gospel message, truth and relevance are the two
indispensable wings on which it is borne. When these twin characteristics are combined, the message soars to its supreme height because it
is deeply earthed in reality.

Yet if one were to talk to a typical skeptic today, the skeptic would
question at least one of these characteristics. How often have we heard
someone muse, "Ah! It just does not stand up to the test of truth." Or
someone else may dismissively opine, "I just do not find it relevant."
Anyone who knows the engaging nature of the biblical message knows
full well that it is not that the message defies rationality, but that the
critic has fled from reason or the communicator has failed in the
demands of meaningfully carrying the message. As far as the critic is
concerned, a careful examination of the cultural mood reveals that it is
not just the message of Jesus Christ that has been evicted from reality
in this postmodern world of ours, but truth as a category. The communicator of the gospel message can very easily demonstrate this. But the
flip side, as far as the communicator is concerned, is that we have frequently made the costly mistake of assuming that if we speak the same
language, we are readily understood.

FRAMING THE GOSPEL

The message of Jesus Christ is immensely profound precisely
because it addresses life with the power of truth while recognizing why
there is resistance to it. Properly presented, it lays bare the predicament
of the heart that resists its claims. Thus the message goes beyond language, in terms of mere speech, and reveals language as a disposition of
the imagination and culture. So while the language may be the same
within a culture, what often changes is the filter through which it reaches
the average listener's ears. Unless we understand the filter, we will be

speaking in garbled terms to those caught in this mix of a high-paced life and a thinking that has become muddied by the instruments of the age.

Let me illustrate. When one looks at a television screen, regardless of its size, the picture is framed by the parameters of that screen. One may be looking at a twenty-eight-inch screen, a large thirty-six-inch screen, or what is now considered a wide-screen home theater model of more than sixty inches. Whatever the size of the screen, *that,* in effect, becomes the frame. But the viewer has involuntarily bought into something else that is happening—the *circumscribing* of his or her thinking, which is far more subtle and seductive than the physical size of the screen. Something in the very nature of the medium makes it a "truth bearer," even if the message is not actually true. Everyone knows that the medium itself is so cold that it takes extra "heat" to bring the needed effect. Everything has to move at a rapid pace. Humor has to be at the rate of a few jokes a minute. The drama has to exploit violence or sexuality, the reason being that it energizes a lifeless medium by shock or exaggeration. Now, one can even watch two programs at the same time so that there is at least one with some action going on. I marvel at the violence against the human mind itself that forces it to murder concentration with the eyes wide open. What has in effect happened is that fiction as a medium seems to have a greater impact as "truth" than a truthful medium, which is often seen as a bearer of fiction. This reversal may well be the most deadly slant of our time. Truth has been "framed" by a medium that distorts reality.

This distortion carries a world of conditioning that has shaped the modern mind. "Talking heads" now appear as a cold medium, and "something dramatic," we are told, is needed to bring life to the message we convey. How mundane it sounds to the modern listener to say, "In the beginning was the Word." How much more imaginative it would be for them had it been said, "In the beginning was video." Yet the Lord of heaven and earth has left us a message. This message is rooted in the Word, and we are to make this Word heard and felt to a generation such as this.

With such a challenge, one can safely say that the pastoral call may in fact be the most difficult call to fulfill today. It is at once an unenviable task and an easy target for anyone to hit, but I know of no more important role for the shepherding of the soul in a vagabond culture that ours has become. Properly understood and pursued, the calling and the gift are of pristine value in a society accustomed to counterfeit. Recognizing this challenge, let us take a look at the pastor as apologist.

A WORTHY CAUTION

Before I proceed, I would like to make one very pertinent observation. I make it at the outset because it is foundational, with everything else built on it. The famed pastor and preacher F. W. Boreham has a sobering essay called "A Baby's Funeral." In this essay he talks of a woman frantically walking up and down in front of his home one Saturday morning, and it was evident that she wanted to come in but was reticent to come to the door. Finally Pastor Boreham stepped out to load up his car for a day's picnic with his wife, hoping, of course, that his coming out would make it easier for the woman to approach him. The woman took her opportunity and went up to speak to him.

It didn't take long for her heartrending story to burst forth through her tears. Her baby had just died, she said. She did not belong to any church and desperately needed somebody to perform the funeral. Boreham got all the particulars, including the name of the father, which she rather hesitantly gave, and all the other information needed to arrange for the burial. He would call on her the next day. He sensed there was more to this story than she had let on. When he returned home that evening, she was outside his door waiting for him.

"I did not tell you the truth," she said. "I had to come back." The baby girl had been born out of wedlock and born terribly deformed, with only "half a face." She had lived a few fleeting minutes and died. "I just need somebody to help me give her a dignified burial. Will you do that for me, sir?"

Boreham's heart was deeply torn by the obvious pain of this story, and he offered any help he could.

In his essay Boreham describes the funeral, attended by only one friend. The baby was laid to rest in the midst of a terrible rainstorm in a brand-new cemetery. Everything about it spoke of desolation and death.

At this point in the essay, Boreham switches scenes and tells of another time when he was on a train journey with the district superintendent of his denomination. At every station where they stopped, a small group of pastors would be there to meet the superintendent, and he would listen to them tell of the challenges and struggles they experienced in their small and varied congregations. No matter what the scenario, Boreham recalled that the superintendent would always end by saying to them, "Just be there for them." Amid their tears and joys, "just be there for them." Amid their struggles and victories, "just be there for them." As he heard the superintendent's words, Boreham said that this woman and her baby's funeral suddenly came to mind. Many years had passed since that baby's funeral. Yet in all those years, there was one person who never missed a Sunday service—the young mother whose baby he had helped bury.

That is pastoring at its core. Pastors are there for their people. They are in the midst of all of their parishioners' emotional strains and successes. This is the best thing pastors can do. Nothing I say from here on will diminish that role. Pastors as apologists have the best apologetic in *their very presence,* and that is a unique privilege.

AN INTERNAL BLEEDING

Everything else buttresses this presence, and it is to that buttressing that I now turn my narrower but pointed attention. Preaching is a vital element of the pastor's call. It is a sacred trust and one that God has chosen as an effective means through which the truths of the Christian faith are uttered. As much as one may bemoan what the pictorial medium has done in commandeering our minds, it is nowhere near the tragedy of what we may have done to ourselves. Many in ministry themselves have come to question the value of preaching. In no other profession would such doubt of its own essential requirement still have been able to survive. Witnessing the triumph of the picture, and what Jacques Ellul called the "humiliation of the word," we, too, have bought into the lie that somehow words are less effective than the visual. I would dare to suggest that few conclusions in society are as dead wrong as that one. The visual may immediately engage the imagination and the emotions, but words are God's primary ordained way of communicating and, may I suggest, a more lasting means of capturing the conscience.

You may recall from Jesus' story of Lazarus and the rich man (Luke 16:19–31) how after the death of the rich man, he cries out in torment from hell for some water to be brought to him. Abraham, at whose side the beggar Lazarus rests, reminds the rich man that the gulf is final. But then comes this plea: "I beg you, send Lazarus to warn my five brothers, so that they will be spared this destiny." Abraham says to him, "They already have Moses and the prophets." "Yes," says the rich man, "but if somebody rises from the dead, maybe then they will believe." Then Abraham makes the startling statement that if they do not believe Moses and the prophets, they will not believe even if someone does rise from the dead. It seems clear to me from this clear utterance that in the eyes of God the word has even a more lasting impact than a mere miracle.

The comforting news is that God has provided both the Word and the miracle, and in like manner, we today can draw both from the hearing and the seeing, but the lasting value is that of the truthfulness of the utterance of God's word. The challenge to find balance without compromise and effect without corruption is immense. For that reason alone, over the years I have learned to respect the calling of the preacher more each day. God, therefore, in his mercy brings us back time and again to the basic nature of communication: "How shall they hear without a preacher?" (see Romans 10:13–15). Part of that preaching requires the enabling of men and women to give a reason for the hope within them (1 Peter 3:15). Apologetics is actually an indispensable component, and anyone who thinks it is not, lives with self-deception. Profound and protracted thought must go into the preparation and delivery of the message that is heard, bringing salvation and deeper commitment to the listener who is stalked on every side by reasons to disbelieve.

WHY THE RESISTANCE?

With so full a responsibility and so huge a challenge, there is an immediate surge of uneasiness within the church leader's heart, and there is a flurry of questions that surface.

First and foremost is this: How amid myriad demands does one keep up with the rapid growth of knowledge? The gigantic leaps in the body of information now accessible to all make the volume of material plainly too vast to comprehend. I remember a medical doctor once saying to me, "I can barely keep up with the literature in *my* field; how can I possibly keep up with *yours?*" I quickly reminded him that the predicament goes both ways. Studying theology is voluminous enough, so how does one keep up with the numerous disciplines represented in any mid-sized congregation of a big city? Most professions afford the luxury of one line of thinking. If I am a biology teacher, for example, biology is my discipline; I am not expected to be a theologian or a philosopher. If I am a philosopher, not only need I not be a scientist, but I have the luxury of being a specialist in just one narrow field to the exclusion of numerous others. If I am a hockey player, I reap the admiration of vast hordes only because I play hockey. If I am a movie icon, I can make any pronouncement on any field and gain a hearing without having had an hour's schooling on the subject. Yet a pastor or active church leader has to know where science is going, build philosophically sound arguments, converse with the sports fans in the congregation, and illustrate sermons from the latest movie. Sarcasm aside, the pastor is under immense pressure to stay abreast of many diverse and often disparate disciplines because the audience is so diversified and the needs are many.

If the first challenge to the pastor and church leader is intimidation before the task due to extraneous demands, the second is a question from within. It is that of uncertainty, if not suspicion. Many in the pastorate, as well as those who hold leadership positions in the church, question the method and the impact of apologetics as it has been customarily used—or should I say misused? We hear it almost as a refrain: Doesn't apologetics focus on the intellect while abandoning the heart? Doesn't apologetics diminish the authority of the Bible itself while exalting reason? Doesn't apologetics end up displacing the role of the Holy Spirit in bringing conviction to the heart? Isn't it a discipline that feeds the pride of the individual? Don't we ultimately accept things by faith? When these queries are added up, apologetics is at best an illegitimate child in the household of faith and at worst a rogue who plunders the wealth of the faithful. No wonder the price is paid by offering a tepid Christianity alongside a scorching secularism.

This combination of a time-demanding discipline and uncertainty within may have left the intellectual challenge unaddressed. But putting the twin concerns in perspective helps bring a correct response to the task of apologetics. To help respond to these concerns, I now turn to the theme of the pastor as apologist and hopefully find some answers in the process.

STARTING WHERE IT MATTERS

The first aspect to be addressed is the character of the apologist. The Scriptures do not divorce the content of apologetics from the character of the apologist. Apologetics, of course, comes from the Greek word *apologia*—"answer," or "defense." First Peter 3:15 gives us the defining statement: "In your hearts set apart Christ as Lord. Always be prepared to give an answer *[apologia]* to everyone who asks you to give the reason for the hope that you have. But do this with gentleness and respect." I have always found this to be a fascinating verse of Scripture because the apostle Peter, under the inspiration of the Holy Spirit, knew the hazards and the risks of being an answer bearer to the sincere questions that people would pose of the gospel. The fact is, when one contrasts Jesus' answers with those of his detractors, it is not hard to see that the resistance is not of the mind but of the heart. Further, I have little doubt that the single greatest obstacle to the impact of the gospel has not been its inability to provide answers, but the failure on our part to live it out. The Irish evangelist Gypsy Smith once said, "There are five Gospels. Matthew, Mark, Luke, John, and the Christian, and some people will never read the first four." In other words, apologetics is often first seen before it is heard. For that very reason the Scriptures give us a clear picture of the pastor as an apologist: one who has first set apart Christ in his or her heart as Lord and who then responds with answers to the questioner and does so with gentleness and respect.

On this issue of character come two immediate imperatives. First, the way the pastor and church leaders' lives are lived out will determine the impact on the skeptic. There are few obstacles to faith as serious as expounding the unlived life. Too many skeptics see the quality of a Christian's life and firmly believe that it is all theory and that there is no supernatural component. I remember talking to a Hindu in the early days of my Christian faith. He was questioning the strident claims of Christians who maintained that Christianity was supernatural. He absolutely insisted that conversion was nothing more than a decision to lead a more ethical life and that in most cases Christianity wasn't any different than other "ethical" religions. So far his argument wasn't anything new. But then he said something I have never forgotten and often reflect upon: "If this conversion is truly supernatural, why is it not more evident in the lives of so many Christians I know?" His question is troublesome. After all, no Buddhist claims his or her life to be supernatural, yet many Buddhists live more consistently than Christians. The same pertains to many of the other faiths. How often do so-called Christians, even while teaching some of the loftiest truths one could ever teach, live a life bereft of that beauty and character?

This call to a life reflecting the person of Christ is the ultimate call of the pastor as apologist. If the shepherd is not living as he or she should be, how can the ones shepherded follow the right path? The skeptic is not slow to notice this disparity and, because of this, questions the supernatural claims of the entire gospel.

The second imperative regarding character is discipline. In the years of seminary education to which the average pastor and church staff member are subjected, the unspoken reality is that for those emerging from the ranks, the future will be determined by how seriously they studied. John Stott, who pastored for many years at All Souls Church in London, England, and authored numerous books on the ministry, made a very simple comment that has profound ramifications. He pointed out that it is reflective of the demise of the pastor's calling when the "Study" is called the "Office." Knowledge increases exponentially, and it is part of our calling to work hard at understanding as much as we can about the themes we must address. Granted, some subjects will elude the grasp of many, but one ought to at least know where the questioner might find help in the area of his or her struggle.

The famed Bible teacher and writer A. W. Tozer had a winning line for those who felt intimidated by the educated. He had just arrived in

Toronto to begin his pastorate after having served for several years in Chicago. Many of Toronto's Christian leaders and other luminaries were present at his "welcome dinner." The man who was going to be his assistant walked around the room, and after looking at the name cards and degrees punctuating some of the names, he walked over to Dr. Tozer and confessed, "I really feel like an ignoramus in a group of such qualified people." Dr. Tozer, as expressionless as he was wont to be while making the most quotable statements, turned and said to him: "Brother Bill, we are all ignorant—only in different subjects." Coming from a man who never went to college and yet touched the spirit of people deeply, it was a worthy reminder.

I am not suggesting that formal learning is unimportant. I am saying, however, that higher education may not be for everyone. Therefore, we must all harness our gifts to the best of our ability, use them with discipline, and study to the fullest extent we can.

In the next chapter I will thus turn to some challenges faced by church leaders today and ask what central tasks leaders should be fulfilling.

QUESTIONS FOR REFLECTION AND DISCUSSION

1. When communicating the gospel, why do you think "we have frequently made the costly mistake of assuming that if we speak the same language, we are readily understood"? How we can communicate more effectively?

2. What phrase, according to the author, summarizes "pastoring at its core," and what do you think this description entails?

3. Describe what the character of an apologist looks like according to the Scriptures.

4. What does the author say has been "the single greatest obstacle to the impact of the gospel," and would you agree with this insight? Why or why not?

Chapter 2

FOUR CHALLENGES FOR CHURCH LEADERS

RAVI ZACHARIAS

A s I said in chapter 1, I have little doubt that the single greatest obsta-cle to the impact of the gospel has not been its inability to provide answers, but rather the failure on our part to live it out. The Scriptures do not divorce the message from the messenger. We are not only called to give answers, but to be answer bearers, often responding with gentle hands and swift feet rather than with words alone.

Recognizing the role that living out a disciplined Christian life plays is a starting point for taking on the responsibility of the work of Christian apologetics. There are numerous tasks one can assign, but I would like to underscore four of them. Years ago, as I began my own journey in this field, it was from the pen of Os Guinness that I learned these truths. I am indebted to him for them. I now take the liberty to expand on them and consider these tasks with the pastor and church leader in mind. Nevertheless, this information could be applied by anyone attempting to handle the responsibility with commitment.

CLARIFY TRUTH CLAIMS

The first assignment for church leaders is to *clarify truth claims.* This purpose is paramount because Christianity has suffered much by flirting with worldly methods and seductions. I well recall delivering a lecture at the Lenin Military Academy in Moscow some years ago. It was one of those experiences when halfway through my own talk I wondered why on earth I had accepted the invitation to speak. I was clearly an unwelcome guest in the minds of many of the officers compelled to sit in and listen. One, in particular, kept giving me the choke sign. Trying to communicate my message through an interpreter with this constant intimidation was no easy task. But as soon as I finished, I realized the almost unpardonable blunder I had made. This same officer sprung to his feet and said, "You have been using the word *God* for the last hour. What do you mean by that term?" My, oh my! How disconnected I had been from my audience. This was a roomful of atheists, and I had not taken the trouble to define my fundamental terms.

We may shake our heads at this unfortunate oversight, but I have come to the conclusion that it is made behind our pulpits all over the world on a regular basis. Even the term *Christian* in many parts of the world today is heard with immense prejudice. In the Middle East, for example, it is almost impossible for one to hear it without its historical baggage and distortion. The claims of Christ are repeatedly made in sermons, lectures, and testimonies, yet rarely do we explain what we mean when we say some of the most basic things. Many listeners have more of a perverted view of what it means to be a Christian than they do an authentic one. Stereotypical answers no longer satisfy.

Os Guinness tells the story of a young protégé of Francis Schaeffer who was sharing his faith with a French existentialist in a Parisian barroom setting. Unknown to the young Schaefferian, the Frenchman had read most of Schaeffer's books. With every answer the Christian gave, the atheist began to see the obvious, until finally he broke his secret and said, "Excuse me, but do you write with a Schaeffer pen, too?" That ended the discussion. Indeed, if the terms are parroted without understanding, the message is garbled and appears inauthentic.

Let me make an important parenthetical statement here. One of the most fallacious ideas ever spawned in Western attitudes toward truth is the oft-repeated pronouncement that exclusionary claims to truth are a Western way of thinking. The East, it is implied, accepts all religions as equally true. This is patently false. Every religion, without exception, has some foundational beliefs that are categorically nonnegotiable and exclude everything to the contrary. You see, truth by definition is exclusive. If truth were all-inclusive, nothing would be false. And if nothing were false, what would be the meaning of *true*? Furthermore, if nothing were false, would it be *true* to say that everything is false? It quickly becomes evident that nonsense would follow.

Even Buddhism, which is often held up as being the example of "religious tolerance," is not exempt from dogmatism. Buddhists forget or downplay the fact that Buddha was born a Hindu and rejected some of the fundamental precepts of Hinduism. Buddha's own statement was that truth mattered more than conformity. What, therefore, takes place in popular thought is a reflection of the way culture has been engineered to deal with truth issues. This is the nerve of the problem in communication. It is the sacred duty of a pastor to remind his people periodically of the very nature of truth, because if truth dies, even at the altar of cultural sensitivities, then so does the gospel in the listener's ears. The first and foremost task of the apologist is to stand for the truth and to clarify the claims of the gospel.

Defending Truth

Clarifying and defending the truth is the hard part of apologetics, because this is foundational. Most people today, when asked to define truth, stumble and stutter because they have never paused to understand what even they themselves mean when they say Jesus is "the way and the truth and the life."

Truth, very simply stated, boils down to two tests: Statements made must *correspond to reality,* and the system of thought that is developed as a result must be *coherent*. The correspondence and coherence tests are applied by all of us in matters that affect us.[1]

When Jesus said, "I am the way and the truth and the life. No man comes to the Father except through me" (John 14:6), he was making a very reasonable statement by affirming truth's exclusivity. The question one may legitimately ask is whether he demonstrated that claim rather than just stating it without any reasonable defense. Hence it is very important when making truth claims before an audience to clarify them. This task is the first and most important step in apologetics.

In one's own preaching, a pastor should be able to defuse most questions. We can illustrate this process by using terminology from the field of electronics. The pastor or leader who stands in the pulpit takes the two prongs of the heart and intellect within the seeker and plugs them into the structure of his or her message, connecting them to the receptacle of God's power that energizes the soul of the recipient. When this happens, the pastor has served as an "adapter" for the need, and apologetics has met its demand. This is the least someone's preaching should do. In answering the questions, the pastor becomes the bearer of God's response.

If the subject is too vast for the pastor or leader to tackle, he or she must find resources or contacts that can help people wade through their questions. Pastors do not have to have expertise in every area, but they must be equipped to point people to resources that will provide answers for their questions. Never before has so much written and videotaped material been available for helping people tackle the hard questions (see the appendix at the end of this book). Well-known exponents deal with issues that young minds grapple with, and in being aware of this material, church leaders demonstrate a cognizance of the issues.

BEAR THE RESPONSIBILITY TO REMOVE OBSTACLES

Second, leaders have a responsibility to *remove obstacles* in the path of listeners so that they can get a direct look at the cross and the person of Christ. This task of apologetics can be equated to what Os Guinness descriptively calls "bush clearing." Here sensitivity to the experience and reasoning of the individual becomes key.

I remember a time in the early years of my ministry when a young couple asked if they could spend a few minutes with me. We sat down and began to talk, and their first question was about the existence of pain and suffering in this world. How could God be a loving God? As I was in the process of answering, I caught a glimpse of their baby sleeping in the pew behind them. I instantly noticed that the little one had been born with some very sad deformities. I then realized that the last thing they needed was an intellectually distant answer to their felt hurt. There were obstacles to their belief in God that could not be set aside by an academic wave of the wand. To enable them to take a look at Jesus Christ without that barrier was the long arduous task of response. Every proclamation necessitates anticipating barriers. And it is only when these barriers are removed by the message and the Holy Spirit brings conviction that the heart can cleave to the cross. Over the years I have witnessed repeatedly what the mature Christian already knows, namely, that ultimately the problems are not intellectual but moral. This knowledge, however, still necessitates a process by which the critic can be made aware of its truth.

Some years ago I was at one of the leading universities of the world. On the second night of the open forums, a student stood up and said to me, "Last night I brought two of the most vocal atheists on the campus to hear your challenge to atheism. They had come ready to attack your lecture, but at the end when you opened it up for questions, they remained silent. So on our way back to the dorm, I asked them why they did not say anything during the time of questions. One of them said that your arguments were pretty tough to counter and held together quite well. I was surprised at their concession. There was silence, and then he added this: 'But we will still remain atheists.' What do you have to say to that?"

The student's question was quite simple to answer. I said, "If you remember my opening statement last night, you will see the point established. I began my lecture by saying that my task was to try to establish that, for most atheists, their atheism is based on a moral problem rather than an intellectual one. They wanted moral autonomy and hence presented their opposition to theism as an intellectual one rather than the other way around. I should therefore consider the point proven." There was silence and then applause from those present. I really did not want the applause, but even a basically divided audience recognized where the problem lay. The task of the apologist is with God's help to help the questioner see his or her own heart as the root of the problem and pray that the Holy Spirit will bring conviction of sin, for that is what it really is. Once this conviction comes and the heart is seen for what it is, the cross stands in its magnificence as the offer of forgiveness.

GIVE SPECIFIC ANSWERS BY CONSIDERING THE QUESTIONER'S WORLDVIEW

The third task for church leaders is to *give specific answers*—and this is essential—*by considering the questioner's worldview.* Here the challenge becomes a little more complex. How does one respond to legitimate fundamental questions and do so with integrity and sensitivity of heart and mind? For example, a teenager may say to her father at the dinner table one evening, "Dad, my social studies teacher told us today that sexuality is basically just a cultural thing and that each culture has established its own terms of right and wrong. Is that true?" What if the father were to say to her, "No, the Bible says there are clear laws that God has put in place for what he intended sex to be." She may well hesitate and respond, "But *my teacher* does not believe the Bible."

The father is right in dealing with the problem for himself, but he puts his daughter in the untenable position of positing a conclusion without defending her source of authority. If the teacher were to name the Bible as the authority, then the issue would be simpler. But if the Bible is denied this place, the father has sent his daughter into the lions' den with nothing to defend her. Therefore I am convinced that the most effective defense of the faith and offense against falsehood must be based on an examination of worldviews and the challenge based on this examination. Over the years of thinking through this issue, I have formed a track of approach with which many have been able to identify, especially as far as preaching is concerned. I call it "The Three Levels of Philosophy."

We must begin by knowing how the mind works and, more to the point, how we must move from thought to action. This demands rigorous practical insight, particularly into the very process by which people come to believe certain things. Some pastors and church leaders may not be given to philosophical thinking, but each of us wrestles with these issues at some level, as surely does our audience.

The Three Levels of Philosophy

A brief philosophical explanation here will help. Philosophy, as I see it in our present context, comes to us at three levels. The first level is the foundation, *the theoretical substructure of logic* upon which inductions are made and deductions are postulated. Put plainly, it depends heavily on the form and the force of an argument. Logic, to most minds, has never overflowed with romance and has seldom triggered excitement. Yet truth has a direct bearing on reality, and the laws of logic apply in every sphere of our lives.

Since the laws of logic apply to reality, it is imperative that these laws be understood if any argument is to stand its ground. This can become a vast subject in itself, but for most purposes, the foundational laws are indispensable to the communication of truth. Peter Kreeft, professor of philosophy at Boston College, has briefly addressed the importance of correct argumentation in his book *Three Philosophies of Life.* In a subsection titled "Rules for Talking Back," he writes the following:

Three things must go right with any argument:

1. The terms must be unambiguous.
2. The premises must be true.
3. The argument must be logical.[2]

In any argument, the application of these rules cannot be compromised if the conclusion is to be defended or refuted. Truth is indispensable to each statement, and validity is indispensable to each deduction. This dual combination is central to the persuasiveness of any argument, and if there is a flaw in either of the two, the argument fails.

This is level one in our philosophical approach, the theoretical realm in which the laws of logic are applied to reality. To deny their application is futile and self-defeating, because one must use reason to either sustain or challenge an argument. In short, level one deals with *why* one believes what he or she believes and is sustained by the process of reasoning, incorporating truth and logic.

For example, I well recall an exchange I once had on the campus of the University of the Philippines in Manila. A student from the audience shouted out that everything in life was meaningless.

I responded by saying, "You do not believe that."

He promptly retorted, "Yes, I do," to which I automatically countered, "No, you don't." Exasperated, he said, "I most certainly do; who are you to tell me I don't?"

"Then please repeat your statement for me," I requested.

"Everything in life is meaningless," he stated again without qualification.

I said to him, "Please remain standing; this will only take a moment. I assume that you assume that your statement is meaningful. If your statement is meaningful, then everything is not meaningless. On the other hand, if everything is meaningless, then what you have just said is meaningless as well. So in effect you have said nothing."

The young man was startled for a moment, and even as I left the auditorium, he was pacing the floor and muttering, "If everything is meaningless, then . . ." And so it went!

The second level of philosophy does not feel the constraint of reason or come under the binding strictures of argument. It finds its refuge in *the imagination and feeling.* Ways of thinking at this level may enter one's consciousness via a play or a novel, or touch the imagination through visual media, making belief-altering impact by capturing the emotions. It is immensely effective, and literature, drama, and music have historically molded the soul of a nation far more than solid reasoning has. Level two is existential and fallaciously claims that it need not bow to the laws of logic.

However, many individuals who take their emotions as a starting point for determining truth, in grabbing the finger of feeling, think they have grabbed the fist of truth. By thinking exclusively at this level, they are driven systematically further inward, until their whole world revolves around their personal passion, with a dangerous self-absorption. They reshape their worldview to a "better felt than tell't" perspective—if it feels good, do it, or, as the line from the song says, "How can it be wrong when it feels so right?" Unfortunately, even many churches have given in to thinking almost exclusively at this level, as evidenced in their worship and preaching. But we shortchange our audience when we divorce our preaching from serious engagement with difficult ideas and instead preach at the level of emotion.

The third level of philosophy is what I call *"kitchen-table conclusions."* It is amazing how much of the moralizing and prescribing in life goes on during casual conversations. The setting can vary from sidewalk cafés, where frustrated philosophers pontificate on profound themes, to the kitchen table, where children interact with their parents on questions that deal with far-reaching issues. The question may arise out of the latest nagging news item or scandal of the day, or it could be a question raised in the classroom, such as the one posed by the daughter to her father. This level of philosophizing escapes neither the child nor the academic dean of a prestigious school, because "Why?" is one of the earliest expressions of human life.

LEVELS OF PHILOSOPHY

Level #3 Kitchen-table conclusions	Why one legislates for the other	Is it transferable?	Application
Level #2 Imagination and feeling	Why one lives	Is it livable?	Illustration
Level #1 Foundation of logic	Why one believes	Is it tenable?	Argumentation

In summary, level one concerns logic, level two is based on feeling, and level three is where all is applied to reality. To put it another way, level one states why we believe what we believe, level two indicates why we live the way we live, and level three states why we legislate for others the way we do. For every life that is lived at a reasonable level, these three questions must be answered. First, can I defend what I believe in keeping with the laws of logic? That is, *is it tenable?* Second, if everyone gave himself or herself the prerogatives of my philosophy, could there be harmony in existence? That is, *is it livable?* Third, do I have a right to make moral judgments in the matters of daily living? That is, *is it transferable?*

None of these levels can exist in isolation. They must follow a proper sequence. Here is the key: One must argue from level one, illustrate from level two, and apply at level three. Life must move from truth to experience to prescription. If either the theist or the atheist violates this procedure, he or she is not dealing with reality but is creating one of his or her own.

Remember the dinner-table discussion between the father and his daughter regarding sexuality and culture? Notice that the father makes his argument at the third level—prescription—while the question comes at another level, namely, Are there absolutes? Therefore, the father must instead establish at level one the reason for, or *reasonableness of*, his claim. He must show that an absolute by nature is not culturally determined. I realize that this is not easily done for people of any age, but it must be done when the mind is capable of engaging the argument.

On one occasion I ran up against this very question from a news reporter. I had just finished lecturing at a university, and she had very graciously stayed through the entire lecture even though she had other pressing engagements. After the lecture was over, she was walking beside me and said, "Can I ask you a question that really troubles me about the Christian?"

I was glad to oblige. "Why," she asked, "are Christians openly against racial discrimination but at the same time discriminate against certain types of sexual behavior?" (She made more specific references to the types of behavior she felt we discriminated against.)

I said this to her: "We are against racial discrimination because one's ethnicity is sacred. You cannot violate the sacredness of one's race. For the same reason we are against the altering of God's pattern and purpose for sexuality. Sex is sacred in the eyes of God and ought not to be violated. What you have to explain is why you treat race as sacred and desacralize sexuality. The question is really yours, not mine. In other words, *our* reasoning in both cases stems from the same foundational basis. You in effect switch the basis of reasoning, and that is why you are living in contradiction."

There was silence, and she said, "I've never thought of it in those terms."

You see, when an argument is taken to the first level, it immediately finds a common point of reference. When it leaps only to the third level, it builds without a foundation.

Church leaders incorporate the components from the three levels in their sermons: the *argument* (or proclamation), the *illustration* (or story), and the *application* (or so what). The Scriptures provide the truth; the arts, literature, or current events provide the illustrations; and the application should go right to daily living. This approach essentially underscores the three levels of philosophy and helps connect ideas with concrete reality.

BRING A BALANCE BETWEEN THE HEART AND MIND

The church leader's fourth task is *to bring a balance between heart and mind*. The danger of getting bogged down on the technical side of debating truth is that one could lose contact with felt needs, and hence the connection must be established. Relevance comes in precisely at the point of application. If, for example, all of the claims of Jesus are backed only by the historical, empirical attestations, someone who struggles only on the existential level will not be able to make the connection. The reason Jesus brings meaning is because of who he is.

People in every generation have lived with various privatized struggles, but today's generations face some distinctive ones. The assault on the imagination by way of the visual has brought with it new horizons but disappointing fantasies as well. Beauty and art have diminishing returns without a worldview to interpret them and fill the gaps. After some time, merely aesthetic or entertaining experiences wane in exhilaration and the mind seeks more. This is the built-in price of pleasure. While the entertainment world may have left one entertained, ever pining for more, the world of knowledge has left old ways of intellectual pursuit on uncertain terrain.

This saturation of the imagination and skepticism of the purely cerebral present an incredible opportunity for the pastor and church leader. Naturalism leaves the spirit unfulfilled, and sheer materialism leaves one weary. The vacuum created by these realities is what has sent Western culture foraging into Eastern spirituality to look for a way to satisfy the spirit. The bottom line is that life has become disjointed though busy, and the heart has become emotionally empty though indulging in every fantasy. The worldview of the average person is an ad hoc way of approaching every opportunity. There is no seamless way of thinking, and the result is a breakdown of life's meaning at its deepest level of need.

The pastor is often the only person who can help people make sense of it all. What a privilege this is! But for a pastor and other church leaders, helping the congregation to connect their fragmented lives and to see the evidence of God's providence involves both the heart and the mind. Even as questions storm the Christian faith and uneasiness attends the role of apologetics, the ministry has sought to find other ways of "meeting needs." Yet such ministry will pay its dues if apologetics is neglected. This is precisely what may have brought about a highly charged emotionalism in contemporary Christian expression, with the mind having been buried in the process. Emotions are a vital part of our being and must be engaged, but emotionalism is the perversion of emotion, jettisoning the reason. As a result, for the average Christian, going to church is just something he or she does in addition to everything else. It is a parenthetical injection into the bloodstream of living, only because the spirit remains undernourished in the harried expressions of daily routine.

The average Christian's trust in the gospel is a "faith commitment" that is necessary to survive, but life itself remains systemically unconnected. Existence becomes a buffet line in which the plate is loaded with what best satisfies the taste; nourishment and moderation are tossed to the winds. Life is filled with plenty of choices, but there remains no unity in the diversity of what we choose. I shall expand on this in chapter 5. For now it is useful to note that the pastor as apologist builds with this unity and diversity in mind.

I well remember a graduate student at Cornell University, at the end of a lecture I gave in defense of the Christian faith, saying this to me: "Every waking moment I am compelled to live within a naturalist framework. How in the name of reason can I make a paradigm shift to the supernatural?" Going to church to have her questions answered was the farthest thing from her mind. She was living a compartmentalized life, yearning for the spirit to be touched, but not thinking that the ministry of the church could provide it. Jesus spoke to the outcasts of society, but fascinatingly, in his selection of two of his most effective spokespersons, Moses and Paul, he picked ones with sharp minds but deep passions. This combination, I believe, must shape our communication so that life is seen as a whole and not as in fragments. In a day when so much goes wrong in many places around the world and so much is spurious, there must be a place where there are answers and where there is integrity in the message. It is the place where God's people are gathered and are shepherded by one who knows how to cross the span from struggle to hope.

WITH GENTLENESS AND RESPECT

Sadly, pastoring is a vanishing vision in our culture. The pastor who comes near has become an endangered species. Amid growth and high-tech ways of communicating, some pastors have become reclusive and distant. For the sake of our culture, I long to see the return of their presence. We must listen to our congregations—and often the *question behind* their questions. When met *with gentleness and respect,* many people admit their vulnerability.

We are called to be faithful in living out and preaching the Word. And God has promised to honor those who honor him. If our preaching leads people to genuine repentance and worship, we will help meet the deepest longings of the heart and mind, and they will find where true discovery lies.

Maybe then the limerick from chapter 1 can be rewritten:

> There was a young student at Trinity
> Who had cracked the square root of infinity.
> But the thrill had its limits
> When just working with digits
> So he went beyond math and studied divinity.

QUESTIONS FOR REFLECTION AND DISCUSSION

1. What is the first task of apologetics? Give an example of how you could accomplish this task or how you have done this already in your ministry.

2. In the third task of apologetics, what is the most effective defense of the faith and offense against falsehood based on?

3. What are the three levels of philosophy? How could you incorporate this apologetic approach in your next sermon or conversation?

4. What do you think the author means when he says, "We must listen to our congregations and often the *question behind* their questions"?

Chapter 3

THE CHURCH AS THE HEART AND SOUL OF APOLOGETICS

JOHN GUEST

This chapter, describing the church as an institution of apologetics, assumes the following statements of the obvious:

- The local church is normally where believers who desire to see their friends come to faith invite them; thus, the local church is the heart and soul of evangelism. That's the way God designed it.
- The business of Christian apologetics is directly related to the evangelistic task. That's the need for it.
- Christian apologetics is not merely the intellectual domain of theological students on their way to a Master of Divinity— although it often seems so. That's the shame of it!
- The church as an institution of apologetics brings together the *rational* and *relational* dynamics of evangelism. The healthy church has both of these. And that's the strength of it.

The church as an institution of apologetics, given her evangelistic task, sees apologetics as an offensive weapon in the hand of each believer, so that he or she can convince unbelievers of the validity of the faith. Apologetics is not just the intellectual defense of the faith so that Christians can feel rationally justified in what they believe. Rather, it is the intellectual persuasion Christians exercise to help others come to faith.

In our postmodern Western culture, skepticism toward the rational process and the rational conclusions we draw is common. Therefore, the quality of the Christian's life, and in particular the Christian community, is an essential part of the evangelistic process. Evangelism today is about existential persuasion as well as intellectual persuasion.

EXISTENTIAL PERSUASION

I have been a believer for more than forty years. For twenty of these years I tried to communicate the gospel to my brother, Anthony. He was successful in business, and while he later acknowledged that he had a real awareness of God, he had given no hint of interest in spiritual things. He never went to church, and he never mentioned faith or prayer.

I invited Anthony and his family to come from our native England to visit the United States. Along with my family, we had two spectacular weeks in Florida. We all had young children, and I explained that we would say grace at meals and that we would be going to church on Sunday. "Respond however you wish," I told him, "but these are our family's customs." As a result, they all went to church services with us and met groups of believers who created a climate in which to hear about Jesus.

At the end of the vacation, just before my brother and his family left to return to England, we came back to my Pennsylvania home. On that Sunday evening I invited a half-dozen people into my home for fellowship around an evening meal. Anthony and I had already played golf a couple of times with several of these friends, so they weren't complete strangers to my brother or his wife. I took the risk that evening of having my friends introduce themselves by telling how they had come to faith in Jesus Christ.

I had no idea what impact that time would have. My brother remembers that evening to this day. It was the most significant part of the vacation, he told me later. How striking that he came from England in

February to Florida weather, stayed on a beach in more than adequate Florida homes, had great times of recreation, yet singled out an evening in my home as the highlight. Why? The spiritual dimensions of that evening had a powerful impact. What he heard from my friends in the intimate setting of fellowship was an essential part of his coming to genuine Christian faith himself. To my delight, Anthony has been a Christian now for twenty years and is active in Bible study and evangelistic programs. His wife subsequently came to faith, and their faith is being passed on to the next generation.

God created the church as the primary institution of evangelism and apologetics. Our culture's bent toward individualism may make us forget it, but what happens in the local congregation and among gathered believers forms the heart and soul of the apologetic task. Whether it is through worship services, evangelistic meetings, small groups, or informal home gatherings like the kind that spurred my brother's acceptance of Christ, the corporate witness of the body of Christ is indispensable.

It is with the local congregation that the Christian meets weekly, after all, so it is there that the quality of his or her Christian faith—for good or for ill—is largely determined. It is to a congregation that believers invite friends whom they want to see come to faith. And it is in the experience of worship that the relational and rational aspects of the Christian meet. There the unbelieving inquirer sees what faith looks like up close and lived out. Congregational life provides the habitat for faith and the heartbeat to our work of giving a reason for the hope that we have.

The unhealthy nature of our social environment today stands in contrast to the health and wholesomeness of the Christian church. The constant barrage of bad news and concomitant existential despair is a negative apologetic for the world, standing in contrast to the positive character of community life in the church. Our "reasons to believe" are all the more plausible because of the perceived reality of a more fulfilling way of life in the Christian community.

The church must never forsake her high, urgent calling to engage in apologetics. Whatever the role of parachurch organizations—and God has blessed them with great fruit—a full-orbed witness requires a gathering of believers, for only in the church can all of God's designs for believers find fruition.

My own experience is pertinent here. As one who has been both a pastor for nearly forty years and an itinerant evangelist for fifteen years, I can say clearly that apologetics as *experienced* in the local church offers the unbeliever far more than an intellectual defense. The church setting provides a richness and depth that goes far beyond mere convincing of the mind. The church and the Christian believer face off against an intellectual skepticism so ingrained in our Western culture that relativism, subjectivism, and existentialism have eroded confidence in rational and reasonable truth. But along with the cognitively grasped reasons for faith, the quality of life in and through the Christian fellowship becomes another powerful, persuasive weapon in the Christian's armory.

While this has always been true, it is all the more so today in this postmodern age when searching and seeking have grown highly visible. Gallup polls provide evidence of this: Three out of ten Americans say they currently belong to some kind of support group; another one in four say they wish they did.[1] Small groups of every kind powerfully shape the life of postmoderns. People find in these groups tremendous resources for the challenges of daily life. As we witness such hunger for communal roots and relational meaning, we are reminded that church fellowship offers what so many hunger for. Church meetings of every kind and size can offer the sense of community and connectedness that people in our age so desperately crave.

Through its corporate life, preaching, teaching, small groups, acts of kindness, even parking-lot conversations, a congregation can winsomely and gently disarm the common distrust of the rational process. It does so in the context of lived, relational reality. It does what no mere individual can do in bringing people to Christian faith.

How can we take full advantage of the church community, with its additional apologetical armaments of love, trust, joy, and purpose, to help bring people to Christ?

WORSHIP AND APOLOGETICS

In her book *Worship Evangelism*, Sally Morgenthaler speaks of inviting unbelievers into the worship of God. The act of people gathering to worship offers a potentially unique experience for unbelievers. By *worship* I mean a vital expression of people loving God through songs and hymns, prayers, preaching that inspires, and fellowship that is enjoyed. Skeptics can thereby witness *existential* as well as *intellectual* persuasion when people gather. They can sense the powerful presence of God.

I have heard of skeptical agnostics entering into such a worship service and for no explicable reason finding themselves weeping as they sensed God's presence. Worship bypassed their normal rational skepticism. God communicated himself to them as the worship of the believing fellowship invoked God's supernatural presence. This same dynamic is present in larger meetings such as a Billy Graham crusade or a Promise Keepers conference. A group meeting in which the Holy Spirit moves and works gives seeking people a taste of another reality. Our unbelieving friends realize that we have other dimensions besides intellect. They become aware of a reality that is beyond immediate, rational explanation. And they thereby become susceptible to the message of the gospel.

Worship also entails a deep experience of community. The quality of the Christian corporate life—the caring that is shown, the needs prayed for, the smiles or embraces or handshakes passed along—all provide potential links in the evangelistic process. Such actions tangibly convey God's invitation to open our lives to the love he has poured "into our hearts by the Holy Spirit, whom he has given us" (Romans 5:5). So the quality of life in the Christian community does more than reassure Christians of what they believe; it also persuades the person whom the Christian seeks to bring to faith. Love is the ultimate apologetic; it reaches the whole person.

One of the most powerful evangelistic tools is the gathering of Christians in a home. Small groups, such as a single family sitting down for devotions or a group of friends gathering for worship, Bible study, and prayer, can communicate profound realities, as my brother experienced. Our simple sharing of our testimonies on that evening helped him become aware of the God we were reverencing. The quality of relationships expressed by people who love the Lord and are endeavoring to relate to one another with integrity, compassion, helpfulness, and honor for God speaks powerfully. Small groups allow people to express an intellectual curiosity in conversations unlike the normal secular conversations of the workplace or social club.

APOLOGETICS IN PREACHING

Sunday morning worship, with the weekly preaching of the Scriptures, is a ready-made classroom for apologetics. The preacher comes with an understanding of the *Word* and an understanding of the *world* to which it is addressed. The gathered people listen together.

Preaching presents congregations with an opportunity to relate truth to practical issues that confront everyone in daily life. This is, again, no merely private enterprise; the Word of God speaks to the whole of life, making sense of life and the issues of society. The Bible, preached into the fault lines of our social structures, gives reasons why the Christian faith makes good sense and provides an apologetic for people saturated (often uncritically) in contemporary culture.

The preacher does this as a regular part of weekly ministry to the people of God and thereby demonstrates, as if in a workshop, applied apologetics. He or she does so in a fellowship of faith striving to make real the gospel's promises and discipleship's imperatives. The burden of the preacher, then, is not just to understand the nuances of the Scriptures through study of language, context, and history, but also the nuances of the culture in which we live by observing advertising, news, fashion, music, entertainment, and decisions in law or government. The preacher then shows how biblical truth impinges upon the culture.

The preacher also remembers that the people in our churches are often bright, educated, and willing to think. We present them with more than clever emotional illustrations and shallow psychobabble in our preaching and teaching. People today can digest strong thought-provoking content and in fact are hungry for it. Our withholding of substantial food for thought has led to an intellectual and spiritual famine.

Decades ago novelist and essayist Dorothy Sayers quoted a former dean of Mansfield College, Oxford, who said, "The tragedy is that all this doctrine, however interesting to theologians, is hopelessly irrelevant to the life and thought of the average man." Sayers responded with these words:

44

If Christian ministers really believe it is only an intellectual game for theologians and has no bearing upon human life, it is no wonder that their congregations are ignorant, bored, and bewildered. It is not true at all that dogma is "hopelessly irrelevant" to the life and thought of the average man. What is true is that ministers of the Christian religion often assert that it is, present it for consideration as though it were, and, in fact, by their faulty exposition of it, make it so.[2]

Given the relativism and subjectivism of much of today's media and education, people starve for content that addresses the issues on the basis of biblical truth. I remember preaching in one very large, well-educated, prosperous Episcopal congregation in Dallas, Texas. I preached for not more than twenty minutes. When I was finished the congregation sprang to its feet and burst into applause! Why? I think it was largely that they were weary of the synthetic pabulum that had been their diet. I also believe it is because the mind is thirsty for the truth, and the Lord Jesus, presented in his own untarnished integrity, is *the* Truth. People are willing to think as long as they sense that doing so will help them encounter something that has intellectual and personal integrity.

A strong apologetic in the pulpit also encourages our congregations to see that deep religious conviction is not just for intellectual Neanderthals, as certain elements in our culture would have us believe. As astounding as it may seem to contemporary skeptics, it is the world around them that has buried its intellect, ostrich fashion! Without apology the relativistic/subjective way of thinking that connotes our culture has "closed the mind" of the average person. Allan Bloom's book *The Closing of the American Mind* gives ample evidence of the incapacity of the American university student (and professors) to think with intellectual integrity or genuine diversity.[3] Meanwhile the Christian dogma is powerfully reasonable. The church is the institution to constantly affirm this. The following are examples of what I mean by this.

Eastern Mysticism

Eastern mysticism has thoroughly infiltrated our Western thinking. With it has come the notion that all religions are somehow saying the same thing and have equal merit. The "circle of life" and reincarnation have also come with this Eastern mind-set. As a way of addressing this whole system of thought, I raise some questions about reincarnation:

- If reincarnation were a fact, and by it people steadily improve in an evolutionary way, becoming more and more morally perfect, would the world not be improving equally and be a better place morally?
- If in the evolutionary moral improvement lies the hope that people are at some point going to improve enough to reach a state of nirvana and not be reincarnated, who do you know who has even come close to that state? Who do you know who is that good? If you know virtually no one, do we not have a very narrow, hopeless doorway of opportunity to reach "heaven" if this theory is true?
- If people were truly evolving to a perfect moral state and leaving this earth permanently so as not to need any more reincarnations, would the world not be steadily depopulating rather than overpopulating? Where are all these extra souls coming from?

Most Christians have never thought through the implications of other religions' inconsistencies. But if lay Christians are to assert and articulate their Christian faith, we must give them the "day-to-day apologetic" to take on the common "day-to-day" conversation of friends who blandly assume that all religions are of equal merit.

Jesus Was Just One of the World's Great Religious Leaders

That Jesus was a good man or a prophet and has no more authority than other religious leaders is part and parcel of this same "nondiscriminating," secular mind-set. C. S. Lewis has best answered this in his book *Mere Christianity*:

> I am trying here to prevent anyone saying the really foolish thing that people often say about Him: "I'm ready to accept Jesus as a great moral teacher, but I don't accept His claim to be God." That is the one thing we must not say. A man who was merely a man and said the sort of things Jesus said would not be a great moral teacher. He would

either be a lunatic . . . or else he would be the Devil of Hell. You must make your choice. Either this man was, and is, the Son of God: or else a madman or something worse. You can shut Him up for a fool, you can spit at Him and kill Him as a demon, or you can fall at His feet and call Him Lord and God. But let us not come with any patronising nonsense about His being a great human teacher. He has not left that open to us. He did not intend to.[4]

In preaching on this issue, we can quote a number of Jesus' "I am" statements:

- "I am the light of the world. Whoever follows me will never walk in darkness, but will have the light of life" (John 8:12).
- "I am the resurrection and the life. He who believes in me will live, even though he dies, and whoever lives and believes in me will never die" (John 11:25–26).
- "I am the way and the truth and the life. No one comes to the Father except through me" (John 14:6).

Then raise the question, as did C. S. Lewis, was Jesus mad when he said these things? Did he deliberately mislead people, knowing that what he said was not true—thereby confirming that he was wicked? Amazingly, you will never find a solitary soul saying that Jesus was mad or deluded; nor will anyone say he was misleadingly wicked! Preaching such simple reductionist thought does three things:

- It encourages believers to be confident about their own faith.
- It gives believers the simple tools for a frank, nonjudgmental discussion on their part, forcing those who have come at the Christian with "patronizing nonsense" to make for themselves the judgment call about the integrity of Christ.
- It forces those who are sitting on the fence of skepticism or doubt in our congregations (and there are many such people) to choose Christ and thereby be evangelized and receive salvation.

As an Episcopal pastor preaching in mainline churches, I have seen fully a third of the congregation in a morning worship service come forward in response to an altar call of surrender to Christ, just by my forcing the issue of Christ's identity. If people cannot draw the conclusion that Jesus was wicked or insane, given the evidence of what Jesus claimed for himself, they are left with only one other conclusion—he was who he said he was—and they gladly surrender.

The Abortion Issue

If relativism/subjectivism is the great intellectual dishonesty of our postmodern culture, then abortion is the great moral aberration. This is most clearly seen in the justification of partial-birth abortion and the lengths to which pro-abortionists will go to protect the choice of mothers and doctors to terminate innocent life.

One Sunday, as the calendar approached the anniversary of *Roe v. Wade,* I stood in the pulpit and asked the following rhetorical questions as a prelude to preaching the Word.

- How can it be in modern, educated, sophisticated America that we can have women marching in the streets for the right to kill unborn babies?
- How can it be that Planned Parenthood fights for the rights of teenage children in our schools to have an abortion without the notification of their parents?
- How can it be that the Supreme Court would use an antiracketeering law to stop legal protests and counseling of women who are on their way into an abortion clinic?
- How can it be that so many churchgoing Christian people are pro-choice, which is pro-abortion, which is pro-death?
- How can it be that a churchgoing president would not stand against partial-birth abortions?
- How can it be that we do not realize that violence in the womb can only encourage violence on the streets?
- How can it be that we do not recognize that when you cheapen the value of the unborn, you cheapen all of human life?
- How can it be that we do not recognize that a suppressed public conscience will callous the conscience of all of us to the indignity done to human life?

- How can it be that condoms are not only made available to school children who are not yet legally of the age of consent, but that condom sale dispensers are being placed in school rest rooms in Massachusetts?
- How can it be that in the commonwealth of Pennsylvania, it is "homicide" to kill a child in the womb by an act of brutality against the mother, but the woman herself, with her doctor, can kill the child by abortion and it can be a legal and acceptable act?

By the time I had finished the last "How can it be . . ." a nearly full apologetic had been starkly challenging the obvious irrationalities of our day, setting the stage for a straightforward apologetic from the Word of God for the sanctity of human life.

All Religious Roads Lead to Heaven

"Jesus is only one of the ways to heaven," you often hear said. To face this issue head-on without attacking other religious viewpoints, I raise the simple issues concerning the claims of the Gospels: If there really is another way to God, which avoids the necessity of Christ dying on the cross in agony for the sins of the world, then God is not "good"; he is wicked! The Lord Jesus on the night before he was executed, made the request, "My Father, if it is possible, may this cup be taken from me. Yet not as I will, but as you will" (Matthew 26:39). If there was a way in which the Father could have avoided Jesus' sacrificial death and ignored that way, then God is not good and he is not love; he is capricious or uncaring.

I go on to preach that I would not want to know a God like that! This again, as an apologetic, forces the reasonable conclusion that if it was necessary for Jesus to die for my sins, then there is no other way to the Father. No other religion even claims such a Savior. So in the words of the apostle Peter before the Jewish Sanhedrin, "Salvation is found in no one else, for there is no other name under heaven given to men by which we must be saved" (Acts 4:12). And when Jesus said, "I am the way and the truth and the life" (John 14:6), he really meant it.

But ultimately our preaching and teaching needs to point out two immense truths:

- The battle for the minds of men, women, and young people is a spiritual battle and not merely an intellectual one. Prayer is the God-given spiritual weapon that must accompany a good apologetic.
- The real issue is not intellectual but moral. Those resisting the gospel may use a plethora of intellectual objections to the Christian claims on their lives, but you can pretty much count on it that the apparent intellectual skepticism is a smoke screen to avoid dealing with the immoral lifestyles or ideas they loathe to relinquish or change.

I remember being in Cincinnati, Ohio, and spending an entire evening with a university student discussing at a pretty sophisticated level the "apologetic" for the Christian faith. Finally, after watching him make evasive move after evasive move, I asked him, "Are you involved in a sexually immoral relationship?" He just smiled and nodded affirmatively and acquiesced to the real nature of his problem. It was an issue of immorality, not incredibility!

CLASSROOM APOLOGETICS

We can never give in to the irrationalism of our age—the post-modern denial of truth. The way this surrender is often expressed in the church is a happy contentment with an exciting worship experience that moves the emotions at the time but has a nearly complete disconnect from the daily life and the cultural discourse it involves.

Just as preaching can and should have an apologetic edge, it needs to be accompanied by systematic teaching in a classroom context. For the church to be an institution of apologetics, we in leadership must call for more serious engagement of our people. This is an immense challenge given the demands already made on them to survive in today's very busy world.

Fortunately, much of the work has been done for teachers and pastors. I draw attention to four very helpful tools for teaching and encouraging apologetics at the day-to-day level of the average educated layperson. For more information on these books, turn to the appendix at the back of this book.

1. *The Case for Christ* by Lee Strobel is "a journalist's personal investigation of the evidence for Jesus."[5] The great strength of this book is that the author is not the "omni-expert," but in newspaper fashion he approaches his topics as a journalist, interviewing experts in a variety of fields. Strobel, a former investigative reporter, uses illustrations from his crime reporting to unlock the closed doors of contemporary thinking. Then by way of an investigative/interview format, he brings a variety of expert witnesses to walk through these doors with well-researched, well-presented information that states the case for Christ. I do not know of a better work at the popular level.

2. *Darwin on Trial* by Phillip Johnson and *Darwin's Black Box* by Michael Behe are two of the best apologetic works on creationism.[6] The ongoing scientific discussion as to whether there is a "created order" in the universe or whether we human beings, along with everything else in existence, are the products of "random chance" is a constant hot topic of debate in day-to-day life. Evolution is taught as a scientific fact in our schools, and creationism is banned. The skeptic easily concludes that if we human beings got here by accident via a process of billions of mutations over billions of years, then God must be fiction. The work done for us by Johnson and Behe is quite extraordinary and gives great intellectual ammunition for apologetics in the fields of evolution and creation.

3. C. S. Lewis was a prophet to our generation. He taught at both Oxford and Cambridge universities in England. His education raised him to be an agnostic of atheistic proportions. His coming to faith was a monumental intellectual struggle. He describes dragging his feet one evening up the stairs to his room at Magdalene College, Oxford, having surrendered to the claims of Christ as "England's most reluctant convert." His writing, intended to help persuade other reluctant potential

believers, is prolific. His *Mere Christianity* is a classic statement blending philosophical reason and moral imperatives with the claims of Christ.[7] Ahead of his time, in particular, he tackled the ever-present relativism, which he foresaw would become so destructive.

4. *More Than a Carpenter* by Josh McDowell is a brief but classic statement of the uniqueness of Christ.[8] He uses to great effect the same reductive process as C. S. Lewis, forcing the reader to a conclusion about Christ. McDowell analyzes Christ's claims under the headings of liar, lunatic, and Lord and drives the thoughtful person to determine which of these best describes him or her.

STRATEGY FOR THE CHURCH

The difficulty is to get well-thought-through and wonderfully usable apologetics into the hands and minds of Christians. The most successful strategy I have found is to gather a group of key leaders from the congregation and convince them of their own need for training and their need to recruit others for training. Simply advertising the classes and inviting people in general to attend is rarely successful in creating a movement. Leadership begets leadership, and recruitment by the pastoral team of the leaders who will move the congregation to follow must be specific and intentional.

I remember preaching the need for witnessing and gathering a few people (by general invitation) to train them. Then via one of my laymen who took Evangelism Explosion training at Coral Ridge Presbyterian Church, I realized how ineptly I was proceeding. Once I grasped the problem, the solution became straightforward. I took myself and four other ministry staffers to Coral Ridge Presbyterian Church to be trained in a weeklong session on how to share our faith. On returning to Pittsburgh, I urged each of us to recruit two key leaders each for a morning class and another two each for an evening class. Our recruits had to have three essentials:

- They had to be leaders/influencers.
- They would train for seventeen weeks.

- They then would recruit two others each and train them for seventeen weeks.

The exponential growth changed the church from the inside out.

5 ministers training 20 people = 25
25 training 50 = 75
75 training 150 = 225

The numbers were not quite as recorded here, but you get the idea. The key was trained staffers recruiting key leaders who could attract other key leaders for training. Any ministry needs a similar strategy to make a difference of any consequence. We have in our churches bright believing people waiting for such a movement. The work of apologetics has been done. The need in our society is apparent. The church sits ready and waiting to get the job done.

CONCLUSION

In the church's preaching and teaching, we must help our people understand the background against which they convey and communicate the gospel, and then we must urge them not to feel discouraged when what appears to them to be perfectly good reasoning comes up against some stiff resistance. This is where the church as a worshiping, encouraging community is so crucial to the whole task of evangelism.

The healthy church as an institution of apologetics has the advantage of being an explanation of the gospel by its very presence. The quality of life in a gathering of believers is a startling apologetic to a world that is critical, negative, competitive, and skeptical. Within the larger context of the local church, a broad variety of personal accounts of how dignity has been restored by the gospel and how marriages have been put back together by the grace of God stand in contrast to the apparent distress in the workplace and classroom. Add to this a code of ethics that works and a sense of belonging on the one hand and of purpose on the other.

The end of apologetics is not simply to bolster the credibility of the Christian faith for the believer, but rather to break through the incredulity of the unbeliever. And while there is overwhelming reasonable evidence for the Christian faith, because in the postmodern world reason is suspect and moral and spiritual values have been reduced to relativistic opinions, the existential power of the healthy Christian community is a powerful apologetic (maybe even more influential initially than any intellectual construct we have to offer). It's as though the truth of the gospel must be existentially perceived—at least initially—rather than rationally grasped.

I am not speaking of a make-believe church. The churches that are successful in drawing people to faith exhibit a tangibly different quality of life that authenticates the message preached. We know there are churches (too many of them) that do not exhibit the joy of the Lord or the intimacy of relationship that Jesus has described as normative. No amount of well-argued reasons for faith can bridge the existential gap that is created by a lifeless, despondent church.

QUESTIONS FOR REFLECTION AND DISCUSSION

1. What does the author mean when he suggests that "evangelism today is about existential persuasion as well as intellectual persuasion"?

2. The author asks, "How can we take full advantage of the church community, with its additional apologetical armaments of love, trust, joy, and purpose, to help bring people to Christ?" How do you respond to his question?

3. Interact with the quote of Dorothy Sayers about the diminished role of doctrine in the church and its seeming irrelevance to laypeople. Do you agree with her assessment? Why or why not?

Chapter 4

The Priority of Apologetics in the Church

Peter J. Grant

Several factors may lead a pastor to minimize apologetics in the ministry of the church—not the least of which are the many other needs that demand his or her attention. As a pastor serving a growing church, I can well understand the pressure felt when other priorities displace apologetics. It is not easy to engage in the study and skills of the apologist when urgent requests are made in person and via cell phone, e-mail, voice mail, fax, and pager! Most laypeople face similar pressures and feel even less inclined than the pastor to delve into apologetics. Compound this with Christians who already feel uncomfortable witnessing or having to defend the faith, and an aversion to the apologist's approach can quickly grow within the church.

Additionally, the minimal role of apologetics in most churches has led believers to feel that apologetics is an intrusion into the real ministry of the church. Whenever a pastor or church does something different from the average church (and creating a vital role for apologetics *is* different), the innovation will be criticized. Attempts by the pastor or leadership to raise the profile of apologetics, to teach apologetics, or especially to address the real questions of unbelievers in the main services of the church are guaranteed to draw criticism and complaints. Any pastor who wants to give apologetics its biblical place in the church must be ready to face and resist these challenges and to teach the truth with conviction. Restoring the biblical role of apologetics requires leadership, dedication, and a deep conviction that God's fundamental call to pastors is to nurture the life of the church and to address the needs of the world.

APOLOGETICS IN THE CHURCH

In the New Testament Jesus told his disciples, "You will receive power when the Holy Spirit comes on you; and you will be my witnesses in Jerusalem, and in all Judea and Samaria, and to the ends of the earth" (Acts 1:8). From what we know of the early church, it is abundantly clear that apologetics was at the heart of their ministry as witnesses. The New Testament church leaders went about their mission as they "argued with," "discussed with," "persuaded," and "convinced" their hearers, whether in the synagogue or marketplace.[1] It is worth noting, however, that only those who were filled with the Holy Spirit did this; that is, the Holy Spirit, active in the lives of believers, affected the way they presented the case for Christ. For example, the book of Acts records this:

> Paul entered the synagogue and spoke boldly there for three months, arguing persuasively about the kingdom of God. But some of them became obstinate; they refused to believe and publicly maligned the Way. So Paul left them. He took the disciples with him and had discussions daily in the lecture hall of Tyrannus. This went on for two years, so that all the Jews and Greeks who lived in the province of Asia heard the word of the Lord.
>
> God did extraordinary miracles through Paul, so that even handkerchiefs and aprons that had touched him were taken to the sick, and their illnesses were cured and the evil spirits left them.
>
> *Acts 19:8–12*

When the Holy Spirit filled the early Christians, he not only moved in them to teach the word of God to believers and to perform miracles (Acts 19:10–11), but he also moved in them to engage boldly with unbelievers by "arguing persuasively about the kingdom of God" (verse 8). The apostle Peter teaches that a consequence of setting apart Christ as Lord is that we are always prepared to give an answer to everyone who asks us to give the reason for the hope that we have; and "gentleness and respect" are to characterize our dealings with unbelievers (1 Peter 3:15). Furthermore, Jude tells us we are to "be merciful to those who doubt" (Jude 22).

When the Holy Spirit fills an individual today, and when the Spirit is truly leading a church, his effect will be evident in the active and loving engagement of a lost world with the persuasive message of the gospel. A Spirit-filled pastor will find opportunities to engage in a reasoned defense of the faith and will ensure that his congregation is likewise equipped to do so. This equipping may be accomplished through seminars, study groups, church school classes, or teaching at the main services of the church. Another idea is to start a specific ministry focusing on apologetics; in most churches a number of people are usually gifted and called to serve in this area.[2]

A pastor should also address throughout his or her messages the tough questions raised by unbelievers or make them the focus of a complete series. A pastor would not go far wrong in taking the chapter headings of this book or the companion volume *Who Made God?*[3] and turning them into a Sunday morning series. At Cumberland Community Church, we do an annual series titled *Reasons to Believe: Beyond a Reasonable Doubt,* or something similar. Our most popular series was titled *God, I Have a Question,* in which we dealt with a different question each week (for example, "Is the Bible Reliable?" "What about Suffering and Evil?" and "Is Jesus the Only Way?") and then opened the floor for a question-and-answer session. Often the way in which the pastor responds to unbelievers is as critical as the content of the teaching; effective apologetics is knowing how to handle the questions and the questioners. The very questions we think we are answering for unbelievers often clear up years of doubt and uncertainty for believers as well!

Jim Petersen, international vice president for the Navigators, pioneer of the Navigator ministry in Brazil—and participant in similar ministries in other countries—as well as author of several books on

evangelism and discipleship, speaks eloquently of the needs of the unbeliever:

> When a non-Christian begins to study the Bible with you, one of his
> biggest unspoken questions will be, "To what degree will I be able to
> express what I really think with him? What will be the reaction if I
> express my true doubts and questions?" The person will first send out
> some rather "safe" trial questions. How we react to these questions will
> affect the level of communication between us from then on. If we
> respond with dogmatism (which is a form of insecurity) or with defen-
> siveness (which is another form of insecurity), the non-Christian will
> quickly understand the rules of the game and will proceed accordingly.
> He will either operate within our limitations—or he will disappear.
> But if we demonstrate an attitude that encourages the expression of
> doubts and questions, our effectiveness will be far greater.[4]

The pastor and church that learn to use apologetics in its proper
place will find that it becomes a very effective handmaiden to evangelism. The philosopher Jean-Jacques Rousseau once declared, "Christianity started when the first village idiot met the first village con man."
Ever since the Enlightenment, a growing culture of skepticism and cyn-
icism has created a kind of "cultural chasm" that keeps unbelievers from
the cross.[5] The cultural chasm is real—unbelievers generally have a negative view of the gospel and its proponents. They believe it to be irrelevant and its message negative. Its perceived "exclusivism" is despised
by a culture that values tolerance above all things (and yet only toler-
ates fellow pluralists).

We as believers know that the gospel is the power of God for salvation and that sharing the gospel is our ultimate goal. Too often, however, we neglect to see the intellectual, emotional, volitional, and other
issues—the cultural chasm—that the unbeliever must navigate before
coming to a place where he or she can or will hear the gospel. Apologetics attempts to help unbelievers negotiate the journey to faith in
Christ—to get beyond the cultural chasm and to face the "cross" chasm
so that they can hear the clear message of the gospel. Even in a postmodern world, clearing up misunderstandings about God, the Bible,
the deity of Christ, the problem of pain, the church, and so on helps
this process. Without effective apologetics, an unbeliever hearing the

gospel may seem unusually indifferent, resistant, or hesitant. Once the prejudices and questions of unbelievers have been addressed in a safe environment, evangelism often becomes the much simpler task of letting people respond to what they have already come to believe.

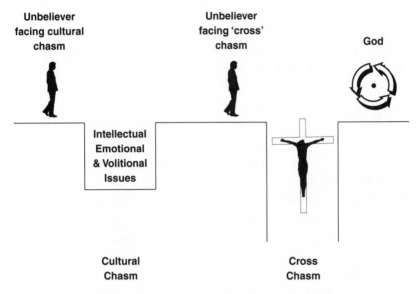

Figure 4.1. The Cultural and Cross Chasms[6]

This chapter deals not so much with the difficult questions that arise from genuine intellectual objections to a particular belief, but with the challenging questions about life that might hinder the process of someone's becoming a Christian. Such questions or objections often have a strong experiential and emotional component. If unanswered, they result in general confusion and resistance to faith in God. They usually involve the perceived futility of human existence, the nature of doubt and faith, and issues of personal suffering.

WHAT DOES IT ALL MEAN?

One of the toughest issues the unbeliever faces is the question of life's purpose and meaning. The Bible addresses this search for meaning throughout its text; in particular, the book of Ecclesiastes looks at life "under the sun"—or life lived without reference to God. Such an existence is deemed "Meaningless! Meaningless! . . . Utterly meaningless! Everything is meaningless" (Ecclesiastes 1:2). Ecclesiastes concludes, however, that living with God in the picture gives that picture new meaning.

Before a pastor or other church leader can share the truth of the gospel or even turn to the Bible, however, he must often show that he is sympathetic to the search and can answer this most basic of spiritual questions. A well-formed answer will lead to an opening to share the gospel; a trite response will close the door.

The unbeliever needs to understand that if human life resulted from blind chance or "an accidental collocation of atoms," as philosopher Bertrand Russell claimed, it would be impossible to derive meaning from it. As the Christian writer and philosopher C. S. Lewis pointed out, "Atheism turns out to be too simple. If the whole universe has no meaning, we should have never found out that it has no meaning: just as, if there were no light in the universe and therefore no creatures with eyes, we should never know it was dark. *Dark* would be without meaning."[7]

Further, meaning simply cannot result from events of accidence. For example, suppose you were passing by our church, and a flock of Canada geese on their way south passed overhead. Suppose you watched in amazement as they were "buzzed" by a small model plane and their feathers fell into the parking lot to spell a message that read, "Come inside to meet the president of the United States of America" (however improbable this may seem). Would you have any good reason to assume that such a message had meaning and that the president truly was inside? No! It was a chance event, so it cannot have meaning. No meaning was put into it, and so no meaning can be extracted from it. The problem is apparent for those who believe that the world and human life began by chance: if no meaning was put in, then no meaning can be taken out. If, however, you had not seen the geese and yet came across the message in the parking lot, you would assume that someone had put it there, and that by following the instructions you would be able to meet the president.

The Bible tells us that the message of God's existence has been written into the universe. In Psalm 19 David tells us that the heavens declare the glory of God: they pour forth speech, they display knowledge, and their words are heard universally (see Psalm 19:1–4). In Romans Paul reminds us, "What may be known about God is plain to [men], because God has made it plain to them. For since the creation of the world God's invisible qualities—his eternal power and divine nature—have been clearly seen, being understood from what has been made, so that men are without excuse" (Romans 1:19–20). When we "see" God's revelation of himself in creation, it can lead us on to a relationship with him. To develop the analogy above, the "feathered message" would not be the only evidence that the president was inside the building and meeting the public. Other evidence would lead to the same conclusion—the presidential helicopter in the parking lot, Secret Service bodyguards at the doors, friends coming out and describing their meeting. Acceptance of the message woven into the universe of God's existence is confirmed in the Bible through the life of Jesus Christ, for example, and through the testimony of those who have met him. The question of meaning leads to the originator of meaning.

It is also worthwhile to point out that the Bible gives us a *personal* explanation for the creation of life and the universe. Every event has both a personal and scientific explanation; science is good at answering the *how*, but each event also needs an answer to the *why*. If I came home to find a broken garage window with a baseball lying nearby, I would ask my son, "Colin, why is the window broken?" If he said, "Dad, it's obvious; an object weighing about 6 ounces and traveling at 30 miles an hour met a 4-millimeter-thick plate-glass window at an angle of 90 degrees—the window broke!" I wouldn't thank him for the Einstein impression. Instead, I would insist on the personal explanation. Likewise, although unbelievers may want to argue the scientific explanation for the origin of life, we would better serve them by focusing on the personal explanation given in the Bible.

Genesis is not primarily a scientific explanation as to *how* life and the universe started, but a personal explanation as to *why* it started. Although everything that the Bible affirms as scientific fact is true, science is not the main purpose or the main message of the Bible. Even if we could work out *how* God did it, we would still need to know *why* he did it. Paul reminded the Athenians at the Areopagus that God "made the world and everything in it," that it is he who "himself gives all men life and breath and everything else," that "he determined the times set for them and the exact places where they should live," and that all this was done "so that men would seek him and perhaps reach out for him and find him" (Acts 17:24–27). Paul started with what his hearers would understand—a discussion about the God who gives meaning to all they see and experience—but he uses it to lead to the gospel: "Now what you worship as something unknown I am going to proclaim to you" (Acts 17:23). The pastor or church leader as an apologist who learns to respond to tough questions about the meaning of life will likewise find that these very questions are a bridge to the gospel.

WHAT ABOUT DOUBT?

Another struggle for unbelievers is understanding the nature of faith and doubt.[8] Church leaders and pastors must be able to help them identify their doubts and recognize how they can move beyond unbelief and doubt to faith. When it comes to faith and doubt, misunderstandings, misconceptions, and caricatures abound. One such example is found in the movie *Miracle on 34th Street,* after Susan, the little girl in the lead role, has met Kris Kringle, whom she believes to be the real Santa Claus. Susan's mother is skeptical of her daughter's belief and attempts to dissuade her from such a false notion but in doing so proclaims, "Faith is believing in things when common sense tells you not to!" Other false notions are that faith begins where fact leaves off, that faith is having 100 percent certainty and doubt is anything less than 100 percent certainty, and that faith is a mysterious gift that has been granted arbitrarily to some but not others.

First, it is worth clarifying that doubt is really uncertainty and is not always a bad thing. If I were to stand beside an empty swimming pool and decide not to jump because I doubted that it was filled with water (and it was indeed empty), my doubt would save me from making a costly and painful dive! Doubt is a lack of certainty about the facts or lack of readiness to take a step of faith based on the facts. In matters of faith, Gary Habermas, chairman of the Department of Philosophy and Theology and distinguished professor of apologetics and philosophy at

Liberty University in Lynchburg, Virginia, describes doubt as "a lack of certainty concerning the teachings of Christianity or one's personal relationship to them."[9] This lack of certainty can come from intellectual, emotional, spiritual, or volitional issues. In his book *In Two Minds,* Os Guinness writes the following:

> The Latin word for doubt, *dubitare,* comes from an Aryan root meaning "two." To believe is to be "in one mind" about accepting something as true; to disbelieve is to be "in one mind" about rejecting it. To doubt is to waver between the two, to believe and doubt at once, and so to be "in two minds."[10]

Doubt can be a form of double-mindedness, always wavering back and forth between belief and unbelief. Most people recognize this as something they want to avoid. The role of apologetics can be to help them address the reasons for their uncertainty and make a decision based on the facts.

Second, if doubt is uncertainty about the facts or lack of readiness to take a step of faith based on the facts, then the solution to doubt starts with *evidence*—answering the questions and ascertaining the level of certainty the facts provide. To return to the swimming pool illustration—if I became convinced through a preponderance of good evidence that there was water in the pool, then my doubts would be cleared up, and I could choose to jump in or stay on the side. I could check the facts before deciding to jump in; the evidence in support might be that I noticed the water line at six feet, I measured the depth with a long stick, I watched others swimming in the pool, I saw someone else jump in, I stuck my big toe in, and so on.

Christians who do not understand the role of apologetics often behave like a man trying to convince a friend to jump into a pool—except the friend believes the pool is empty! Many unbelievers are enormously relieved to know they can process their doubts before jumping; in fact, doubts about the evidence and the decision to jump can be treated as separate issues. The evidence presented in this book (and others like it) can be the best place to start for someone standing on the side of the pool.

After Jesus' resurrection the disciple least certain about the fact of Jesus' resurrection was Thomas. Thomas doubted, but his doubt eventually led him to confess Jesus as "My Lord and my God" (John 20:28). Thomas was willing to express uncertainty about the facts—"Unless I see . . . , I will not believe" (verse 25). But what seems like doubt is sometimes faith in process—"Unless I see . . . , I will not believe" can also mean "If I see, I will believe." Faith is often stronger when arrived at via the valley of doubt. Thomas was rewarded with a personal appearance from Jesus and an invitation to check the wounds in Jesus' body—"Put your finger here; see my hands. Reach out your hand and put it into my side" (verse 27). Jesus was presenting Thomas with the evidence he needed to believe. Sometimes seeing is believing! Unbelievers need to be treated as genuine doubting Thomases and presented with the evidence they need to answer their questions. At the same time, they must be challenged to acknowledge, "If I see, I will believe." We can encourage them to "hedge all their bets" in praying something like this: "God, if you exist (and I don't yet know if you do), and if Jesus is your Son (and I don't yet know if he is), and if you can forgive my sins and send the Holy Spirit to live in me (and I don't yet know if you can), please show me and lead me to you." I have encouraged hundreds of unbelievers to pray such a prayer and then rejoiced with them later as they trusted Jesus Christ. I know God honors such a prayer; I prayed it myself as a young agnostic after reading C. S. Lewis's book *Mere Christianity*.

Third, doubt can also be an absence of faith for which the solution is a commitment to believe. Continued doubt in the light of knowledge of the facts is often revealed as simply unwillingness to believe. As one wit has put it, "God often can't be found for the same reason a thief can't find a policeman—he's not really looking for him!" To go back to the swimming pool analogy, I may still choose not to jump despite overwhelming evidence that the pool is full. This illustrates the difference between doubt as an absence of facts (for which the solution is evidence) and doubt as the absence of faith (for which the solution is *a decision to believe*).

There is a volitional element to faith. Jesus addresses Thomas after presenting the evidence by saying, "Stop doubting and believe" (John 20:27). Thomas had said, "Unless I see . . . , I will not believe" (seeing is believing), but after presenting the facts, Jesus essentially said, "Unless you believe, you will not see" (believing is seeing). The truth is that we can't see what we won't believe. If Thomas had refused to believe at this point, he would have revealed that he was not *unable* to believe but was *unwilling* to believe; his lack of faith was no longer uncertainty or honest doubt but unbelief. C. S. Lewis comments in *Mere Christianity* that no one could ever learn that two plus two equaled four if they approached that fact unwilling to believe but expecting to find out. Faith is like trust—it must be acted upon to become actual.

Apologetics as the handmaiden of evangelism must lead to a clear presentation of the gospel. After all, the only cure for blindness is not information about the *possibility* of seeing but instead sight itself! David Watson makes a similar point in his book *My God Is Real:*

> Unless we are born again, we cannot see the kingdom of God. A man once stood on a soap box at Hyde Park Corner, pouring scorn on Christianity. "People tell me that God exists, but I can't see Him. People tell me that there is a life after death; but I can't see it. People tell me that there is a judgment to come, but I can't see it. People tell me there is a heaven and hell, but I can't see them. . . ." He won cheap applause and climbed down from his "pulpit." Another struggled onto the soap box. "People tell me there is green grass all around, but I can't see it. People tell me that there is blue sky above, but I can't see it. People tell me that there are trees nearby, but I can't see them. You see, I'm blind!"[11]

Finally, it is worth emphasizing to unbelievers that some doubts are processed best in the context of a relationship with God. Unbelievers will sometimes cling to the view that they cannot make a decision to believe in the face of any doubts at all. This notion, however, ignores the central truth that Christianity is a *relationship* with God, not a religion. For example, if I see my wife going into a restaurant for lunch with another man, I may have questions about why she would do that without telling me—and indeed I would want to know who he was! Some would even doubt their wife's faithfulness. But our relationship is so strong that I would not be plagued by these doubts nor even allow them to keep me from my relationship. I would go to the source and ask my wife, who could clear up all doubt for me. If, in fact, the man was her distant cousin who had come into town unexpectedly,

I would have clarified my doubt with the facts and strengthened my relationship.

Doubt dispelled through good communication within the context of a loving relationship is the key to a strong marriage, just as it is to strong faith—but I first must enter the relationship. I enter marriage by saying "I do" to the question "Will you take this woman to be your lawfully wedded wife?" I enter a relationship with Christ by saying "I do" to the question "Will you take this God-man to be your Lord and Savior?" Again, effective apologetics prepares the way for the truth of the gospel.

Likewise, the pastor or church leader as an apologist needs to beware of raising more doubts than he or she answers or of failing to cut a clear path to the cross! For example, if it were my job to convince you that my wife gave birth to a baby girl in 1993, I could provide all kinds of evidence to convince you of this—pictures of my wife before and during her pregnancy, the sonogram telling us we were having a girl, receipts for her maternity clothes, hospital records for her stay in the maternity ward, a copy of the birth certificate, and the birth announcement we sent out. I could also introduce you to eyewitnesses—the doctor and nurses who helped deliver Fiona—and let you speak to my family in Scotland, whom we called within hours of the birth to announce the good news. You could dismiss each single piece of evidence (the birth certificate may be a forgery, the witnesses may be lying to cover for me, and so on), but the evidence taken as a whole proves beyond a reasonable doubt that my daughter was born. In the same way, while no single argument will convince an unbeliever of God's existence, the weight of evidence will lead the unbeliever to conclude that God does exist.

In trying to prove my point, however, I may miss the single most convincing argument and proof that my wife gave birth to a baby girl in 1993—I could introduce you to Fiona today! The greatest discovery an unbeliever can make is not just that God is *real* but that he *really* wants to know us. The pastor who waits for all arguments to be settled before sharing the gospel does a disservice to apologetics. We are not arguing a set of facts but arguing the facts so that a relationship might begin with the living Christ who can, by his Spirit, invade the human soul and grant the gift of eternal life!

WHAT ABOUT THE BAD TIMES?

Suffering, trials, and tragedies also seem to offer a barrier to faith, and some unbelievers will hold back from faith in God because of some hurt perceived to have come from the hand of God. A pastoral response, informed by good apologetics, can address the emotional and spiritual barriers to faith that find popular expression in phrases like, "After that, I couldn't believe in God anymore," or "That was when I lost my faith." Good pastoral counseling means knowing how to deal with such comments from unbelievers and using the opportunity to present the gospel.

The first idea to establish is that we are *spiritual beings* and, as such, need to interpret our physical circumstances in light of spiritual realities. Teilhard de Chardin, French paleontologist and philosopher (1881–1955), once said, "Man is not primarily a physical being having a spiritual experience but a spiritual being having a physical experience." This truth is vital in seeking to convince those with a grudge against God.

A man who had recently started attending our church called me to request a meeting. He was a hardworking thirty-nine-year-old father of two who recently had been diagnosed with inoperable, untreatable brain cancer and had sought to "find religion" in the midst of his tragedy. His problem was that every priest, minister, therapist, or counselor he had spoken to (and he had spoken to many) built up the idea that his cancer was the biggest problem in his life and counseled him on handling his anger. He railed against God as I listened, and he turned silent as I told him that the biggest issue he had to face in his life was not the tragedy of cancer but his need for a relationship with God— tough as that was to do! I reminded him, "You are not primarily a physical being trying to have a spiritual experience, but a spiritual being having a physical experience. Your physical experience is tragic and very hard to deal with, but you have had no choice over your physical experience—whether or not you got cancer. You do, however, have a choice over your spiritual experience. What God wants to offer you is eternal life—a quality of life that only God can give, a life that can start here and go on forever—and it is your choice as to whether or not you receive this gift from God. You cannot blame him for an unsatisfactory physical experience when it's the very thing that got your attention so he can offer you an eternally satisfying spiritual experience."

The man quickly conceded that he had never once in all of his counseling been challenged to think this way. Within a few minutes of my sharing the gospel with him, he confessed his sins and asked Christ to be Lord of what remained of his physical experience here on earth. A few months later I conducted his funeral. Amid much grief, I had the privilege of reminding his family and friends that on the basis of Jesus' words in John 5:24, he had not crossed over from death to life a few days before the funeral, when his physical experience came to an end, but a few months before the funeral, when his spiritual experience took on a new dimension and he received the gift of eternal life.[12]

Another barrier to belief is the idea that some tragedy or trial resulted in one's losing his or her faith. The truth is that tragedies and trials can build our faith or reveal our lack of faith, but rarely will they cause us to lose it.[13] Many who think they have "lost their faith" are actually discovering that they never had any real faith to begin with. Before a newly built ship is launched, it is taken for sea trials—a storm is vital for an effective test. The purpose of the trials is not to destroy the ship but to reveal any defects in the ship's seaworthiness. A building is granted a completion certificate after extensive testing on its electrical, heating, ventilation, and air-conditioning systems, as well as on its pipes, elevators, and other equipment. It does not lose its suitability for occupancy; rather, the tests reveal whether it was suitable in the first place. Likewise, when God tests us, we cannot lose what we never had. Tests do not make us lose our faith; tests reveal our faith or lack of it. It is easier to persuade unbelievers to embrace something they have never had before (real faith) than to try to help them re-embrace something they "lost," which in fact was a false hope and failing them anyway.

Unbelievers will often refer to terrible tragedies that have happened to others (for example, the Holocaust, wars, the Columbine shootings, and the September 11 terrorists attacks) and comment, "I can't believe in the goodness of God after things like that." I usually counter by saying, "I can't believe in the goodness of man after things like that! It's not God whom I lose faith in when tragedies happen; it's man. God's solution is the only antidote to man's evil choices."

I am reminded of the story of a wise pastor counseling a distraught young college student who announced, "I have decided that I cannot and do not believe in God!" He replied, "Describe for me the God you don't believe in." The student proceeded to lay out all his doubts about God and his charges against God. When he finished, the pastor responded, "Well, we're in the same boat. I don't believe in *that* God either."

Simmering beneath the surface of such hot issues is the question as to whether tragedies are a way in which God deals with us. Jesus answered the misconception that those whom tragedy struck were necessarily either worse sinners or guiltier than those who had not suffered (see Luke 13:1–5). He also reminded his listeners that, more important, all within hearing needed to repent, for they too would most certainly perish—an example of Jesus' teaching his followers that their spiritual experience was of greater importance than their physical experience. We look back for a cause or an explanation, while Jesus looks forward for a purpose. In a similar incident, when the disciples asked who had sinned, thereby causing a man to be born blind, Jesus replied, "Neither this man nor his parents sinned, but this happened so that the work of God might be displayed in his life" (John 9:3).

Even believers need to be encouraged when struck by terrible tragedy as to what true faith is. Faith is not having the answers to our suffering (the book of Job teaches this!). Faith is *trusting God despite our suffering*. Several times I have counseled mature believers who have gone through divorce, bereavement, or other trials, and in their discouragement—even depression—they have doubted all the truths they once held dear. Some question why they are facing trials at all. In no way should we minimize the great pain and grief some will suffer in this life, but instead tell them that, as Larry Crabb says so well, "Finding God in this life does not mean building a house in a land of no storms; rather, it means building a house that no storm can destroy."[14]

Some are overwhelmed by grief or pain and cannot reconcile their circumstances with what they previously believed about God. Often they are embarrassed that they are not better witnesses or cannot offer more answers to those who may go through similar trials. They are caught up in the present as though it is the future; yet faith is "being sure of what we hope for and certain of what we do not see" (Hebrews 11:1). I often ask these believers, "Assuming that God helps you through this trial, and assuming that you come through it being comforted by God, would you be willing to comfort others with what you have learned?"[15] Almost everyone answers, "Yes!" This, too, is faith.

The truth is that everyone can choose to be strengthened by faith or to be weakened by doubt through suffering. Most will agree that, as the old saying goes, "when the clock runs smoothly, we forget the clock-maker." Pain is, as C. S. Lewis said, "[God's] megaphone to rouse a deaf world."[16] When we suffer, sin's effects, just as much as intellectual doubts, turn us against God rather than to him. The ultimate answer to the question of suffering is the cross. As much as we might like to ask, "Why does God allow suffering?" our real problem is sin, and our real question ought to be "Why did God allow Jesus to suffer on the cross?"

CONCLUSION

When it comes to the ministry of apologetics in the local church, the pastor and other leaders must know the way and show the way. They must lead the church by conviction and example in helping people answer tough questions about life. In teaching and leadership they must equip believers to give reasonable answers. They must help unbelievers to see that questions of meaning, doubt, and suffering can help them to move from asking God, "How can I know you exist?" to "How can I know you?" The pastor who ignores the role of apologetics in dealing with these questions will find himself offering compassion without conviction and comfort without the ultimate comfort of knowing God; he will leave his hearers stranded in a sea of doubt and miss opportunities to share the gospel. The words of Paul to Timothy serve as a powerful reminder for pastors:

> In the presence of God and of Christ Jesus, who will judge the living and the dead, and in view of his appearing and his kingdom, I give you this charge: Preach the Word; be prepared in season and out of season; correct, rebuke and encourage—with great patience and careful instruction. For the time will come when men will not put up with sound doctrine. Instead, to suit their own desires, they will gather

around them a great number of teachers to say what their itching ears want to hear. They will turn their ears away from the truth and turn aside to myths. But you, keep your head in all situations, endure hardship, do the work of an evangelist, discharge all the duties of your ministry.

2 Timothy 4:1–5

QUESTIONS FOR REFLECTION AND DISCUSSION

1. What is the biblical basis for using apologetics in the ministry of the local church?
2. Why is the existence of God the best answer for someone on a search for meaning in life?
3. In what different ways might we understand and respond to doubt expressed by the unbeliever?
4. How might we respond to those who believe that some trial or hardship has hindered their faith?

Chapter 5

ARROWS AND SWORDS
IN THE CHURCH

RAVI ZACHARIAS

The early church father Origen, in his commentary on Psalm 36, made this observation:

> All in whom Christ speaks, that is to say every upright man and preacher who speaks the word of God to bring men to salvation—and not merely the apostles and prophets—can be called an arrow of God. But, what is rather sad . . . I see very few arrows of God. There are few who so speak that they inflame the heart of the hearer, drag him away from his sin, and convert him to repentance. Few so speak that the heart of their hearer is deeply convicted and his eyes weep for contrition. There are few who unveil the light of the future hope, the wonder of heaven and the glory of God's kingdom to such effect that by their earnest preaching they succeed in persuading men to despise the visible and seek the invisible, to spurn the temporal and seek the eternal. There are all too few preachers of this calibre.[1]

The description is a pointed one, if I could be pardoned the pun, to refer to the evangelist as an "arrow" of God. I do wonder, though, if Origen were alive today, would he mourn more the scarcity of the effort or the toughness of the task? I have no doubt that in some parts of the world, the calling and even the possibility of fulfilling the calling is uncommon. But where there is an abundance of effort, I see more of a challenge in how best to be effective in communicating the gospel message than I see the absence of the opportunity to communicate it. The question is important. How does one preach the gospel throughout a lifetime and retain a freshness of the message? Facing this challenge presents extraordinary disciplines.

But in a real sense, that difficulty is not altogether new. C. S. Lewis, in his book *The Screwtape Letters,* has the senior devil giving advice to the junior devil on how to weary the listener when he or she hears the gospel. Lewis puts his finger on the pulse of this reality: "Work on their horror of the Same Old Thing. The horror of the Same Old Thing," says the senior devil, "is one of the most valuable passions we have produced in the human heart."[2]

Those are sobering words. When good news becomes dreary news, how does one stir the passions without changing the news? My wife tells of the time when she and her sisters were still quite young and were taken by their parents on a family vacation. On a Sunday they were in an unfamiliar church but nevertheless chose to attend Sunday school. The teacher began his lesson in a rather dramatic fashion, giving a few clues of the personality he was talking about. And then, with great melodrama and gestures to match, in a stage whisper he inquired, "And guess who that is?" There was silence, and he spat out the words, "The apostle Paul!" My wife's younger sister groaned, "Not him again." She was sure they had traveled too far to still be haunted by the "same old story."

As humorous as her reaction was, she gave an indication of how the human mind deals with familiarity. How often we ourselves, as preachers, lose the power of the message only because we have heard it so often! The horror of the same old thing is that chronic bent of mind that takes away from the glorious message that brought us to Christ and reduces that very message to appear as of no value.

THE CHALLENGE TAKEN TO HIGHER LEVELS

It's not hard to understand the short life span of enthrallment for a child. But the danger of sophisticated minds attacking the relevance of biblical truth is a far more serious problem. Some time ago I was reading an article by Arthur Peacocke, a renowned scholar at Oxford University. Peacocke directs the interdisciplinary program in the study of religion as it relates to science. He is a highly respected professor, a recipient of the Templeton Prize for Religion, and he often provides some very worthy material for those interested in his field. In the article he called the church to task with regard to the nature of its message and its proclamation. But, quite shockingly, in a conclusion I must deplore, he pleaded with the church to change not merely its approach to the contemporary mind-set but also the very message of the gospel. He made this observation:

> To be truly evangelical, the church of the next millennium will need a theology that will necessarily have to be genuinely liberal and even radical, particularly in its relation to a worldview shaped by science. For Christian theology to have any viability, it may well have to be stripped down to the newly conceived essentials, minimalist in its affirmations; only then will it attain that degree of verisimilitude with respect to *ultimate* realities which science has to *natural* ones—and command respect as a vehicle of public truth.[3]

One marvels at such an unabashed assertion that in effect denies the very supernaturalness of the message of Jesus Christ. Think of the task to which he calls us: a Christian theology "stripped down to the newly conceived essentials, minimalist in its affirmations." How ridiculous of one who has such superb thinking skills to reconfigure the Christian faith as something to be manufactured rather than recognizing it as something revealed by God in his Word. I have news for this scholar: What he wants is a Christianity that is not biblical and one that loses the very reason for its power.

The implication of Peacocke's plea is that man has come of age and can no longer buy some of the "basic stuff" of the gospel message. He is wrong, dead wrong, both philosophically and empirically. If we were to face the truth, the more we see the unconscionable ends to which the human spirit has descended—while bragging of intellectual gains—the more we see how impoverished the human condition is. This scholar would do well to remember the caution offered by the noted English journalist Malcolm Muggeridge: "All new news is old news happening to new people."

And so into this age-old human predicament of building earthly kingdoms, Jesus brought a different and dramatic—albeit radical—response to the need of the human heart. His response is a mystery to us because we are engulfed in spiritual blindness and seduced by the idols of our own making, playing the ultimate game of deceiving ourselves into thinking that we have progressed. There is ultimately only one antidote to our predicament—the glorious display of God at work within a human soul, bringing about his work of restoration and equipping to live for the kingdom of God. Such a transformation begins at the cross. God's answer was a stumbling block then, and it is a stumbling block now. Only if it is properly and seriously understood can its beauty be seen.

THE POWER OF THE MESSAGE

The heart of the gospel is the cross of Jesus Christ. The cross stands as a mystery because it is foreign to everything we exalt—self over principle, power over meekness, the quick fix over the long haul, cover-up over confession, escapism over confrontation, comfort over sacrifice, feeling over commitment, legality over justice, man over God. In the cross alone pain and evil meet, and in the cross alone love and justice are found. Upon both love and justice we find our moral and spiritual home. If only one of these two is focused upon, an inevitable perversion follows. The ideals of liberty, equality, and justice taken in a vacuum have led to ideologies with dastardly experiments left in their wake. And love unbounded by any sense of justice demands commitment without accountability. In the cross of Jesus Christ, the restraint of justice was met and the generosity of love was expressed.

The pastor who proclaims this unique message by word and deed becomes the sword of the Spirit—indeed, as Origen wrote, an "arrow of God"—bringing a counterperspective to a world that clings to rights without understanding wrong. The pastor as evangelist, therefore, revels in the distinctiveness of Jesus' offer and relies on the regenerative power of God's Holy Spirit. This is our calling and our commission in being witnesses for him.

In two remarkably powerful passages, God contrasts his Son to two very notable proclaimers of his truth (see Matthew 12:38–42). The first is Jonah, an unwilling prophet, who nevertheless was heard by the Ninevites, resulting in a national revival. The second is Solomon, whose utterances carried such depth of wisdom that even the heathen came from all over to hear him. Jonah and Solomon, two great names in the Old Testament—yet we are told that Jesus was greater than both of them. In Jesus the message and the miracle, the wisdom and the power, combine. If the lesser had hearers, why would we not want to carry the greater, for the salvation of the whole world, and realize that there will be an audience for that truth? Through his word and his being, Jesus is the changer of the human heart. By our willingness and by preaching, what wonderful miracles of transformation might be wrought?

DEFINING THE TERMS

Who is an evangelist? One who will "herald the good news of God in Christ." At the risk of sounding trite, God's heart is that of an evangelist. He is not only the subject of the Good News, but he longs to see this Good News through the agency of the human voice penetrate with conviction into the human heart (see Romans 10:14–15).

The New Testament words *euangelizomai* and *euangelizō* render this very meaning. Before the New Testament period had ended, the term *evangelist* had come into common use, signifying the worker whose task was announcing the good news to those who had not yet heard or believed. The noun appears in Acts 21:8, referring to Philip the evangelist, and in Ephesians 4:11. We see the specific role listed as one of the gifts to help build up the body of Christ. Finally, in 2 Timothy 4:5, we find the familiar charge of Paul to Timothy to "do the work of an evangelist."

Unquestionably, the task of the early church to evangelize was a rigorous and demanding one, and to help accomplish it, some persons were divinely selected to focus on that ministry. It is also important to note that the "pastor-teacher" was placed alongside those who had the gifts of an evangelist, hence retaining the distinction of that office. Of course, it may be argued that all preaching should ultimately proclaim the gospel, and in this sense the pastor as evangelist is not a separate and distinct role but an essential part of the pastor's calling. In taking a look at a pastor's calling, we can get a good understanding of how the role of the evangelist is taken on also by the pastor.

An important point must be made at the outset: Evangelism is done not only in public proclamation but also in private conversation. This fact is often overlooked, and one may be particularly susceptible to this oversight when considering evangelistic preaching. Let us not forget our personal responsibility. The pastor, however, has the supreme responsibility in the local church to make sure that the gospel is clear and distinct and that it is the reason for the church's coming into being. There are several such means to ensure that the gospel goes forth.

PREACHING AS EVANGELISM

The method God set for evangelism is proclamation of his holy Word. Systematic and regular exposition of the Scriptures provides necessary knowledge for persons considering the truth of the gospel and essential instruction for living out the truth. Origen's word for the evangelist was *arrow*. God's own description of his Word is *sword* (see Ephesians 6:17; Hebrews 4:12). One may wonder why such militant terms are used, but if we realize the hostility with which the Word is often resisted and the Enemy of our souls who seeks to counter it, clearly for the Word to penetrate us it must conquer strongholds in the deepest part of our beings. It is "that word above all earthly powers," of which Martin Luther wrote in his hymn "A Mighty Fortress Is Our God." Luther also wrote this stanza:

> And though this world with devils filled,
> should threaten to undo us,
> we will not fear, for God hath willed
> His truth to triumph through us.

The prince of darkness grim,
we tremble not for him—
his rage we can endure,
for lo, his doom is sure:
one little word shall fell him.

The effective power of the Word taking root in an individual's life brings understanding and repentance. In the process of systematic exposition, the text on hand provides the reason for emphasis. There is a natural flow of content when the Word of God is expounded line upon line, precept upon precept.

In North America the approach to evangelism is sometimes misguided in its attempt to "tell it all" in one mere sermon. Understandably, the evangelist bears this burden because his or her task is precisely that—to present the gospel with his or her unique anointing and particular calling and often in one sermon. But in the pastoral role, time is a component with a different weight. Having repeated opportunities to share the gospel, the pastor can sometimes dwell on just one aspect of it, knowing that it is a foundation on which the rest will follow. If evangelism can be seen as building a bridge, and each sermon a span, then each sermon need not be the entire structure.

One may well argue that the audience may not be there for the completion of the bridge and therefore should have the whole story told at every opportunity. Obviously an opportunity may be accorded for heartfelt consideration in each presentation, but this is not the same as a comprehensive exposition in every sermon. Even Jesus waited for the appropriate time before getting to the demands of the gospel message. The truth is that many a heart needs this preparatory time before the seed is planted. Forcing every text to "tell it all" is not wise exposition.

One of my Old Testament professors during seminary days was blessed not only with fine expository and oratorical skills but also with a sharp wit. Among his witticisms that stand out in my memory is one he repeated a dozen times each semester as he waxed eloquent on the need to return to genuine expository preaching: "Keep your finger on the verse." By this he warned the would-be preacher not to stray from the passage under study. While that reminder was as clear as a bright sunny day, the dark clouds of despondency would descend upon the student-preacher who finished his or her sermon and sat down to await the professor's verdict. The moment of truth would arrive as the professor mounted the platform, leveled his gaze at his meekly seated victim, and said, "Great sermon; poor text." The indictment brought anguish, indicating without apology that the ideas that had been expounded, though wonderful, had not emerged from the text.

All presenters of the gospel must heed this educator's caution. Often audiences are subjected to a barrage of ideas that betray more the pet peeve or preoccupation of the speaker than they do the intention of the text. Any text wrenched from its context is in danger of becoming a pretext. Who of us is not familiar with the discomforting ploy often used in prayer meetings where the objective of a prayer is to stab the conscience of someone within earshot rather than to touch the heart of God? As certain as we are that the intention of such a prayer is woefully wrong, so equally certain we may be of the fallacy of an exposition that has nothing to do with the text.

In the systematic exposition of God's Word, the gospel will sometimes emerge in its full-fledged bloom and at other times as a seed. In some traditions in which the preaching plan follows the "Christian calendar," there is a legitimate time of the year when the memory of a "truth in season" is brought into focus. The lack of a system promotes prejudice and imbalance. For this reason alone the great task of exposition ought to be a gift highly valued and nurtured, exercised through all of Holy Writ, so that God's message will be heard and treasured.

PREACHING TO THE SKEPTIC

When one studies the finest exponents of evangelistic preaching in Scripture, the apostle Paul stands out as the quintessential example of how to cut across cultural lines and philosophical bents without compromising the message. This was brought home to me some time ago during a visit to Greece. To this day, at the base of Mars Hill is a huge bronze plaque with the words of Paul's address to Stoics and Epicureans, memorialized for us in Acts 17. Paul began with this statement:

> Men of Athens! I see that in every way you are very religious. For as
> I walked around and looked carefully at your objects of worship, I even
> found an altar with this inscription: TO AN UNKNOWN GOD. Now what
> you worship as something unknown I am going to proclaim to you.
>
> *Acts 17:22–23*

Paul's point of entry was where his listeners were in their own thinking; and while his goal was to expose their intellectual failure, he began by affirming their spiritual hunger. Step by step Paul proceeded from their need to the one who is omniscient—God as revealed in Christ. Christ alone was the answer for both the weak and the strong. Paul was keenly aware of his context, and with compelling relevance he applied the truth of the gospel and won a hearing. Some influential men and women made their commitment to Christ that day, and the church was established in Athens on firm footing. In fact, one is quite taken aback to see the name of the main street that runs alongside Mars Hill. It is named after Dionysius the Areopagite, who made his commitment to Christ at the end of Paul's message. Two thousand years later the hill and the street stand as a tribute to a message and its recipient.

From Athens Paul moved on to Corinth, a dramatically different setting. New Testament scholar William Barclay notes that Corinth was a wicked city: "The very word *korinthiazesthai,* to live like a Corinthian, had become a part of the Greek language, and meant to live with drunken and immoral debauchery." The word *Corinthian* came into the English language to describe in regency times "one of the wealthy young bucks who lived in reckless and riotous living."[4] Any reader of Paul's epistles to the Corinthians is familiar with the catalog of such vices, ending with the words, "And that is what some of you were" (1 Corinthians 6:11). But one is immediately arrested by Paul's opening words to them: "I was with you . . . not with enticing words of man's wisdom, but in demonstration of the Spirit and power" (1 Corinthians 2:3–4 KJV).

As I stood at Corinth I was overwhelmed by Paul's message. There on a marble slab were etched those powerful words of 1 Corinthians 13, possibly the greatest exposition on love ever written. How did Paul apply the truth of the gospel to a people so depraved? It is easy to see. Lofting over the ruins of ancient Corinth stand the remains of the temple of

Aphrodite, the goddess of sensual love. This temple housed a thousand prostitutes who paraded their offerings each night before the insatiable Corinthian passion and pastime. Paul contrasted this vulgar expression of love with the purity and beauty of God's love, which rejoices with the truth and is eternal in nature. With what riveting force these words hold the reader captive today, disclosing the grandeur of love and overwhelming the imagination when read in the context of Corinth's greatest need.

As I reflected much on Paul's approach, I could readily see the potency of truth when conveyed through the framework of one's thought and life. Paul would have made a horrendous mistake had he come to Corinth as he had to Athens, armed with logic and argument. In Athens it was a battle of the *mind*—philosophy. But in Corinth it was a battle for the *body*—sensuality. Yet there is a connection—indeed, an inextricable one. Both the minds and hearts of the hearers must be addressed such that they may be prepared to surrender to the gospel. But let us not miss the point. The way to the heart in each city had to be from a different starting point of the gospel, which culminated in a particular application. In other words, there is great danger in assuming that one approach fits all. Understanding and repentance are the fruit of expository preaching that is met with personal or even national application.

THE BASIC APPROACH
TO PROCLAMATION

From observing Paul's method, I clearly see four necessary components in his evangelistic preaching that we must bear in mind when doing our own—identification, translation, persuasion, and justification.

The Critical First Step

Identification is that effort that works both ways for the communicator. He or she must be able to identify with the mind-set of the listener, even as the listener must be able to identify with the elements being presented by the preacher. So much is lost through prejudice or misunderstanding that what is often rejected by the listener is not the biblical Christ but a Christianity that bears no resemblance to the Jesus it proclaims.

Recently I was visiting a monastery in the Mediterranean region where for centuries a small group of monks have lived in caves, spending their lives in solitude and prayer. As we walked through their library, we were shown that all the literature they were allowed to read was directly from Scripture or their saints. There was, however, a copy of one of Aristotle's books, but it had a danger attached to it. In medieval times that genre of book was laced with arsenic on every page, so that if perchance a monk took it up to read, when he moistened his finger to turn the page, with each touch of the page, arsenic would make its way into his bloodstream and he soon would drop dead "for having ingested worldly knowledge." As well meaning as these monks are, in attempting to speak to God about humanity, they have lost the ability to speak to humanity about God.

How different from the apostle's approach! Paul knew the ideas that shaped his audience and knew well how to harness them to advantage for the cause of the gospel. It is vitally important for the pastor to know his audience. Thus I add to the injunction "Keep your finger on the text" this advice: "and your ear to the audience." To ignore the latter could well elicit the indictment, "Great sermon; wrong crowd." Identification is a critical first step.

From Speaking to Communicating

Translation carries it one step further by putting God's timeless message into timely idiom. Paul well knew that he needed an ideational translation from his worldview to theirs. Is it any different in our time? For example, even a magnificent word like *salvation* carries a narrow idea to the one who does not understand the breadth that salvation brings. Salvation is not just "pie in the sky by-and-by when I die"; it is inherited immediately.

Jesus' message to the woman at the well was translated from her theological smoke screens right down to where she lived (see John 4). In his conversation, he systematically moved her from her past to her present, from the proximate to the personal. Her ecstatic report to her own people was that he knew everything about her (see John 4:29).

John the Revelator used this same translation approach when he worded his message to the church at Ephesus ("I know your deeds" [Revelation 2:2]). Translation carries the burden of words and concepts that do not create gaps but build bridges.

From Communicating to Convincing

Persuasion is the component that locks the listener in with inescapable interest, such that he or she begins to listen with felt need. Often it is the illustration or the story that draws the listener in with riveted attention. One can tell in any sermon when this moment comes. This persuasion ought not to be confused with the persuasion that only the Holy Spirit can bring. But I am convinced that in this step the Spirit of God takes the truth of what is said and lodges it into the heart of the listener. Illustrations of this abound in virtually every listener who has responded at the end of a message.

From Convincing to Closure

The final step is that of *justification*—why what has been said is true and not false. Paul's reference to the resurrection is clearly this aspect in his message to the Athenians (see Acts 17:31). That Jesus attested those claims by his dramatic defeat of death is the ultimate proof that he was who he claimed to be. This logically leads, then, to the invitation to repentance and trust in the offer of Christ's message of forgiveness and life.

The pastor has this privilege in public and in private to build the message systematically and relevantly. But it is here that the pastor's privilege builds beyond that of the evangelist. From preaching evangelistically he or she is able to go to the next step.

MUSIC AS EVANGELISM

Proclamation is one form of evangelism the pastor uses to reach the lost. A complementary mode of evangelism is music. Lyrics and music powerfully combine to reach a generation that thinks with its emotions. It is crucial to understand this.

When music gives voice to the struggles of the people in the pews, the preacher is "given permission" by listeners to go deeper and address the real problem: our sin and God's holiness. It is not that the pastor should put the topic of sin on hold from the pulpit. Rather, it is the listeners who have put this topic on hold and who often don't recognize their sinfulness until the cries of their hearts and minds are addressed in a medium through which they are able to hear.

My own experience testifies to the impressions carved upon my consciousness by popular music. I recall an occasion in my pliable teenage years when I sat in my living room in New Delhi, India, suspended between the dreary world of my physics textbook on my lap and the low sound of music from the radio in my ear. In this "between two worlds" state of mind, I was suddenly captivated by the sentiments of a song that seemed to echo the struggles in my own heart. The strange blend of Eastern chant in the background and the crisp baritone voice of the singer, a westerner, conveyed a sense of universality to the obvious anguish that imbued each line and articulated the questions I had painfully suppressed. The song cataloged all the breakdowns of our world—the broken home, broken dreams, broken promises, and ultimately the broken life. Then the haunting refrain was repeated again and again—"But who will answer?"—and I did not have an answer.

The truth was not new, but the registering of it in my heart and mind was fresh because of the power of music. My conversion to Christ came a couple of years later, and God used those lyrics to reveal to me not only my own emptiness but also the emptiness of a whole generation without Christ. Our times are making of music possibly more than it is intended to be, but we must understand why this is so and how best to use music constructively for the sake of our emotions.

WORSHIP AS EVANGELISM

Finally, evangelism happens in the context of the whole community of God's people engaged in worship. Years ago I read a definition of worship from the famed archbishop William Temple that to this day rings with clear and magnificent tones:

Worship is the submission of all our nature to God. It is the quickening of the conscience by his holiness; the nourishment of mind with his truth; the purifying of the imagination by his beauty; the opening of the heart to his love; the surrender of will to his purpose—and all this gathered up in adoration, the most selfless emotion of which our nature is capable.[5]

The more I have thought of this definition, the more I am convinced that if worship is practiced with integrity in the community of God's people, worship may be the most powerful evangel for this postmodern culture of ours. It is imperative that in planning worship services, the pastor and church leaders give careful attention to every element and make sure that the worship retains both integrity and purpose.

A few years ago, two or three of my colleagues and I were in a country dominated for decades by Marxism. Before we began our meetings, we were invited to a dinner, through some common friends, all of whom were skeptics and, for all practical purposes, atheists. The evening was full of questions posed principally by one who was a notable theoretical physicist. Questions also came from others who represented different elements of power within that society. As the night wore on, we got the feeling that the questions had gone on long enough and that we may have been going around in circles.

At that point I asked if we could have a word of prayer for them and for the country before we bade them good-bye. There was a silence of consternation, an obvious hesitancy, and then someone said, "Of course." We did just that—we prayed. In this large dining room of historic import to them, with all the memories of secular power plastered within those walls, the prayer brought a sobering silence and a recognition that we were in the presence of someone greater than us. When we finished, every eye was moist and no words were spoken. They hugged us and thanked us with emotion written all over their faces. The next day when we met them, one of them said to me, "We did not go back to our rooms last night until it was early morning. In fact, I stayed in my hotel lobby most of the night talking further. Then I went back to my room and gave my life to Jesus Christ."

I firmly believe it was the prayer that gave them a hint of what worship is all about. Their hearts had never experienced it. Over the years I have discovered that praying with people can sometimes do more for them than preaching to them. Prayer draws the heart away from one's own dependence to a position of leaning on the sovereign God. Often the burden is instantly lifted. Prayer is only one aspect of worship but one greatly neglected in the face of people who would be shocked to hear what prayer sounds like when the one praying knows how to touch the heart of God. To a person in need, pat answers don't change the mind; prayer does.

CONCLUSION

Proclamation, music, worship—in my estimation, these are three profound means God uses to communicate to resistant hearts. The pastor often carries the privilege of providing leadership in these areas. The church as a unit gives occasion time and again, within the provision of its fellowship, to meet the needs of lonely hearts. The pastor builds a congregation with this legitimate need in mind.

As one preacher once put it, if we preach to a hurting audience, we will never lack for a hearer. This is well said and true. But there are also many who have become so hardened to their own need and so prejudiced in their own distortion of the gospel that one almost has to make the listener aware of the need before offering hope. It is one thing for a drowning victim who cries for help to be offered a lifeline. It is quite another for one to be swimming out into the deep, quite oblivious that his strength will fail and he will have none left to swim back. To minimize the method to reach such persons is to kill, not to rescue, for unless they are made aware of their desperate plight, they will continue to blindly trust in their own strength and efforts. Or to change the metaphor, it is one thing for the wounded to feel the need for a hand of rescue; it is another for one to feel that his own armor will never be pierced. For the latter, the arrow of God is the answer and the sword of the Spirit the means.

May there be many such arrows in our time, and the world will get the point.

QUESTIONS FOR REFLECTION AND DISCUSSION

1. Reflect on a few opposing ideas (such as "power over meekness") that follow the statement "The cross stands as a mystery because it is foreign to everything we exalt." How does the way of the cross challenge some of our ways of thinking?
2. Describe what the pastor as an evangelist looks like, particularly the idea of being an arrow and a sword.
3. Explain the four necessary components in evangelistic preaching that the author observes in Paul's ministry.
4. Identify the three means of evangelism that are instruments of the church, and elaborate on each of them.

Chapter 6

CREATING AN APOLOGETIC CLIMATE IN THE HOME

J U D Y   S A L I S B U R Y

THE HAND THAT PASSES THE TORCH

Not long ago I was invited to speak at a large national conference in Washington, D.C. Although it wasn't a meeting of church leaders, I think that church leaders might have found it interesting. So let me invite you to listen to what occurred. Why? Because I'm convinced that church leaders have an important role in encouraging the families in their church to set the tone for an apologetic understanding of the Christian faith with their children in the home.

In my breakout session, after the moderator had presented a long introduction, I stepped up to the microphone and stated boldly, "Thank you for that wonderful introduction; however, there is one thing missing: I am also among a group of the most powerful and influential individuals in our country. I'm a full-time homemaker, home-educating mom, who just happens to be totally on fire for the Lord Jesus Christ;

so be afraid, be very afraid." The audience laughed and applauded, and I went on to say, "Now, some might like to convince me that this job is unimportant, but my question is, If it is so unimportant, why do they all want to do it for me?"

Later that evening, during the banquet ceremony, I enjoyed a patriotic musical presentation. I was captivated by one performer in particular, an eight-year-old girl, my daughter Nicole's age, who was singing her heart out for love of God. What struck me the most, and this may sound odd, were her tiny hands holding the microphone. My eyes welled with tears as I thought about my daughter's soft, creamy little hands. Even though it was only a weekend trip, I was missing her.

As I flew home to the other Washington, I kept thinking about those tiny hands clinging to the microphone. But when I thought of my daughter's tiny hands, I pictured them raised high and clinging to a torch—a torch that my husband and I would pass on to her and now also to our new son, Mikael, in obedience to these words from the book of Deuteronomy:

> Love the LORD your God with all your heart and with all your soul and with all your strength. These commandments that I give you today are to be upon your hearts. Impress them on your children. Talk about them when you sit at home and when you walk along the road, when you lie down and when you get up.
>
> *Deuteronomy 6:5–7*

This injunction follows the Ten Commandments and is one of the first stipulations of the covenant that God gives to Moses and his people. Its placement at the outset of the covenant reveals, first, the priority God places on the home. Second, it suggests that if parents are faithful to teach their children well, all God's people will flourish, for the home is a microcosm of a society. Third, the obedience to God's covenant and enjoyment of his blessings set out in the twenty chapters that follow this injunction is founded on parents who love the Lord fully and model this relationship to their children. So as parents it is vital to ask ourselves, Have we neglected to pass on to our children the torch, which carries the Light of the world? And have we taught our children with the same vigor as those who might wish to rob the Light from them?

MISCONCEPTIONS IN PERCEPTIONS

I firmly believe that teaching children to be effective apologists is not only perfectly in line with the admonition of Deuteronomy 6:5– 7, but also with the description of the excellent wife in Proverbs: "She opens her mouth with skillful and godly Wisdom, and in her tongue is the law of kindness—giving counsel and instruction" (Proverbs 31:26 AMP OT). My hat is off to torch-passers, Grandmother Lois and Mother Eunice (2 Timothy 1:5), who apparently taught young Timothy well and are commended for it by the apostle Paul. The challenge today, however, in teaching apologetics to parents is that there are misconceptions in the perceptions of what apologetics means and what it takes to become equipped. Let's take a look at the various ways some parents in your church may perceive apologetics and the task of the apologist.

Apologetics Is About Arguing, and Arguing Is Divisive

On occasion I have wondered, *Why do I enjoy apologetics so much, and why does it seem to come naturally for me?* One reason is that I had been in corporate sales for years. I was accustomed to the responsibility of knowing my product inside and out, giving sound reasons as to why my customer needed my product and why it was better than the competition, and equipping myself with answers to objections before they were raised. For me, arguments were an occupational necessity. The only thing that has changed for me is that my "product" now happens to be eternal life (no warranty necessary)!

Consider for a moment these terms: cosmological *argument,* teleological *argument,* and ontological *argument. Cosmological, teleological,* and *ontological* sound scary enough, and then tacked on to them is this seemingly negative word *argument.* The word *argument* has lost its positive meaning, and people who *argue* are typically perceived as divisive and annoying! In reality, though, arguments are necessary in order to arrive at truth. Just as passion is now confused with anger, constructive arguing is confused with divisiveness. Therefore, you are put in a position where it's increasingly difficult to say to a group of people, "Today we are going to teach you how to offer sound *arguments* for why you believe what you believe."

Apologetics Is Too Hard to Get Your Arms Around

The word *apologetics* sounds strange and lofty; thus, some church members, perhaps some who attend your church, think it is too lofty. Therefore, we also find ourselves in a position of not being able to say to a group, "Today we are going to learn *apologetics.*" Many are not sure what the word means. Some have said to me, "I don't need to apologize for my faith!" Usually, I do not interject this word until about halfway into my presentation, after I've been able to share some basic examples of how apologetics is applied.

Apologetics Is Only Accessible to the Well Educated

Some church members believe that the job of an apologist should be left to those women or men who hold a Ph.D. or Th.D. The reason is that good apologetics material communicated in an easy-to-read manner is hard to come by. Even when parents reach the point of deciding to equip themselves, they can be hard-pressed to know where to start. They wonder just how they're going to communicate the information to their small children.

While J. P. Moreland's *Scaling the Secular City* serves the learned apologist well, a parent who works all day long, whether in the home or outside the home, may not want to scale the book at the end of the day, let alone scale the secular city. We must, as Donald Grey Barnhouse said, "get the hay out of the loft and put it on the barn floor where the cows can get at it." Or, to put it another way, we must put the cookies on the bottom shelf. Books like Josh McDowell's *New Evidence That Demands a Verdict* and Norman Geisler's *When Skeptics Ask* are excellent resources that accomplish this goal quite nicely.[1]

Apologetics Is Irrelevant to Daily Life

The parents in your church may not recognize the value of equipping themselves in the area of apologetics. It reminds me of when I was in the voice-messaging industry. At the time, the technology was fairly new, and many of my prospects had never heard of voice mail or voice messaging. Because of this, my task was to educate my prospects and then explain the variety of ways they could use our service for their business. Once I explained the value and pointed out areas where it could help them, they were interested. But before they realized the value, they thought that the previous way they had handled their telephone calls was good enough.

I have been told countless times, "My life is my witness, and that's good enough." While I agree that our life should be a witness, what happens when our small children ask the one question that becomes a permanent part of their vocabulary from the age of three on? The question, of course, is *Why?* Or what happens when, because of exemplary external witness, neighbors over the fence—or the grocery clerk, the pediatrician, or our children's schoolteachers or guidance counselors—ask why we act or talk in a way that reflects a sense of hope or genuine love for those around us? This is why I believe parents are the most influential individuals in our society. Not only are they incredibly influential in the lives of their children, but they also have the power to influence the numerous people they meet in any given week—if only they'd realize the value of equipping themselves in the area of apologetics.

Another person some parents have the opportunity to meet is the cult member who knocks at their door. I can't even begin to tell you how many of these folks I've had the pleasure of speaking with on my doorstep since I became a full-time homemaker. It is such a pleasure, because I can comfortably engage them for Christ's sake and glory. But for the person who is not equipped, this knock at the door often means drawing the curtains and pretending you're not home, and so disappears another witnessing opportunity.

My daughter loves to hear me speak with unbelievers. She sits and observes, and when they've gone, we talk about what she observed. What kind of testimony do we have if we are always hiding with the children behind the couch? Well, we cannot hide forever, and our children are taking note. If our life is our witness, then we had better start taking the Great Commission seriously. It amazes me how many people I've met who abandoned the faith because their parents never gave them straight answers to their questions, and cult members were all too eager to offer enticing and engaging answers.

Apologetics Is Only about Reaching the Head

Sadly, some parents underestimate themselves intellectually. Yes, they may be too mentally fried at the end of a long day to absorb heavy apologetic material, but of course it doesn't mean they lack the mental acumen to accomplish the task. Nonetheless, parents need much encouragement when given the opportunity to become equipped in the area of apologetics. Indeed it may be one thing for them to rest upon the arguments for God's sovereignty and goodness in a broken world; it may be another thing to convince their child of these truths, especially when he or she experiences rejection or pain. What a challenge for those of us who are church leaders!

I personally have found it a great advantage to be intellectually underestimated, for when people underestimate you, they drop their guard and are more apt to discuss spiritual matters in a nondebate, nonbelligerent format. One apologist friend refers to me as "an apologist with a mother's heart." While he enjoys going for the jugular, he recognizes that my goal is to lovingly move skeptics to my position without them realizing I've done it. We need to reach both the head and the heart, and parents have many unique opportunities, yet none are so impacting as those involving their children.

AS A CHILD THINKETH

When my daughter was about four years old, another mom spent an hour on the phone relaying to me the details of a particular movie she thought was cute—and that I should purchase it for my daughter. My husband and I rented it and watched it to see if it would be appropriate.

The story line was clever and the characters adorable, and it was clear that it would draw children in—until they would find themselves watching a few disturbing scenes. I asked several other mothers what they thought about this movie and about the things my husband and I found troublesome. Each one shrugged it off and said, "My kids have already been exposed to all that. They're used to seeing that kind of stuff." Entertainment subtly desensitizes its viewers; yet, like the frog in the kettle, we are unaware—and the heat is rising.

Before something enters the eye-gate to permeate the thought-life, we are urged by the apostle Paul to pass it through this wonderful guide, test, and filter:

> Whatever is true, whatever is worthy of reverence and is honorable and seemly, whatever is just, whatever is pure, whatever is lovely and lovable, whatever is kind and winsome and gracious, if there is any virtue and excellence, if there is anything worthy of praise, think on and weigh and take account of these things—fix your minds on them.
>
> *Philippians 4:8 AMP NT*

This is not to say, however, that we must avoid thinking about or must turn our eyes away from those who are broken, persecuted, or violated. Indeed, God declared through the prophet Micah that "what is good" and what the Lord requires is "to act justly and to love mercy and to walk humbly with your God" (Micah 6:8). Rather, the apostle Paul suggests that such virtues (notice that they are rooted in the Old Testament) should always inform our thoughts and actions, particularly as we teach our children to discern what is just, true, and good.

I firmly believe in the sponge principle. Small children absorb what surrounds them, both positive and negative, so it's important to consider the impact we can make on our children's thought-lives. Is the priority we place on entertainment damaging our children and the way they process information? We can redeem their thought-lives, and we can repent and ask their forgiveness if we were responsible for allowing their minds to be polluted in the first place. As Christians we are called to a renewing of our minds (see Romans 12:2). We can use God's Word and Christian literature to edify our children's thought-lives and in the process intellectually challenge them. Church leaders can encourage moms and dads to read with their children such books as *The Chronicles of Narnia* by C. S. Lewis or John Bunyan's *The Pilgrim's Progress.*

We want to raise discerning children, and we cannot if we do not carefully examine what they are exposed to, whether through movies or books. I'm not suggesting that we shelter them to the point that we create an unreal environment, but we must help them become so familiar with the pure and good that they can readily spot what is impure or erroneous. The woman at the well knew exactly what Jesus was talking about with regard to her immoral lifestyle, yet Jesus did not give graphic details; he simply defined her relationships. She then said to the men of the city, "Come, see a man who told me *everything I ever did*" (John 4:29, emphasis added).

We can teach our children that, while the Christian life is often difficult (for we are being set apart for God's use and glory), they can be encouraged that God is faithful to give them what they need to handle the trials they will face. We can encourage them that the Christian walk is challenging and exciting as we have an opportunity to live out the book of Acts. And we can show them in creative ways how to do so. Christian bookstores, for example, sell representations of the full armor of God as outlined in Ephesians 6. What a great opportunity a mom or dad has during playtime, as they put a piece of the armor on their small child, to teach the child in a dramatic way why each piece is necessary. Their small child, then, will be actively participating in the learning experience instead of sitting idly by.

Daily the Lord provides teaching opportunities we can seize to answer our children's questions or to help them gain wisdom, insight, and an eternal perspective. I'll never forget one such opportunity I had with my daughter. In spite of the 600-foot drop in elevation, Nicole and I decided to go hiking on the breathtakingly beautiful Harmony Trail in eastern Washington, the only hiking trail that leads directly to Spirit Lake at the foot of Mount St. Helens, where a volcano erupted on May 18, 1980.

As we descended at the beginning of the trail, we were surrounded by lush foliage, beautiful wildflowers, and waterfalls just big enough to create puddles to leap over. Once we reached the bottom, we emerged from the foliage that protected us from the heat and found ourselves in desert-like conditions, barren and flat, a monument to the power of the blast. We were glad we had rationed our water, because in the still air and heat we needed it. After hiking quite a ways, we descended again down steep drop-offs until we finally reached Spirit Lake. Once there we beheld, opposite the exquisite Harmony Falls, a captivating view of Mount St. Helens with its massive crater and lava dome. We took full advantage of the cool (I should say, freezing) water. We talked about God's creative power, majesty, provision, and preservation. We sang praise songs and had a great time together.

Then it was time to head back, which was a bit more difficult. Nicole was less than enthusiastic about the desert-like area and the 600-foot ascent. I encouraged her along and reminded her of the fun we'd had and what we had beheld with our eyes. We were thrilled to see the trail-head sign just ahead—signifying that we had accomplished the task and that an ice-cream treat was in our future. But something very interesting happened, which I believe was God-ordained, something my daughter and I will never forget. In fact, she refers to it whenever we take a hike, whenever we resist the temptation to give up and not keep going.

At the top of the trail, looking down at the foliage, across the barren landscape, and toward Spirit Lake, stood a man with his son, who was probably a bit older than Nicole. After exchanging a hearty "Howdy," the man asked, "So what was it like? Is it beautiful?" We described, as best we could, just how beautiful it was. "Well, we would do it, but we don't have the right shoes for it," he explained. I said, "I definitely wouldn't hike it without plenty of water. It's a little deceiving from up here." He nodded, called to his son, hopped into the car, and left.

"What happened?" Nicole asked in surprise. "Why didn't they do the hike?"

"Baby girl," I said with a huge smile, "They didn't have the right gear, they knew it was difficult, and they weren't prepared. But we were prepared, and even though it was difficult, we were the ones who had the opportunity to see it and tell others. While they can only imagine its beauty, we got to experience it because we were willing and prepared."

Nicole understood instantly and gained a new appreciation for our firsthand experience. We took a moment to thank God for giving us the health and strength to accomplish such a task, and we talked about how we never want to do anything that might damage that gift. So much was taught and learned during that one outing.

Not all parents live near a volcano, but they can visit a park. Perhaps they live in the city. They can take a moment with their child and observe the people and how all are different and unique, each with beauty and a divine purpose. They can ask their small child, "What would you think if I told you there was a great explosion here, and when the dust settled, there were all of these buildings?" This would be a great object lesson for teaching that if it took an intelligent human to design and create the buildings, then there is an intelligent God who designed and created us. We must seize the opportunities to reason with our children on myriad subjects. The point is, we can and should provide our kids with the intellectual gear they need to climb the mountains that will allow them to gain eternal rewards.

Now perhaps you're thinking, *Some parents may not feel very creative and won't think that they can readily spot these teaching moments or find an application for them.* All I can say to that objection is—how big is our God about whom we preach and teach? Mine will give wisdom liberally and without reproach to all who lack and ask for it (see James 1:5). I am living, breathing proof—yet another testimony of the reality of the living God. I fasted and prayed on my face before him that he would grant me the wisdom I needed to teach my children. I cried out to him for help with my studies. I prayed that he would give me the ability to understand and wade through the materials that would help me become equipped, all the while believing he is Jehovah-Jireh—"The Lord Will Provide." He is sufficient to provide not only the opportunities to seize divine teaching moments but also the wisdom and resources to make the most of them.

WHAT'S A PASTOR OR CHURCH LEADER TO THINKETH?

Our postmodern culture has provided us with the greatest opportunity to teach apologetics to our children. Just as it was a small child who recognized that the emperor had no clothes, children will, more than anyone, recognize that moral relativism is stark naked! Listen to children on a playground for five minutes, and what do you hear? "That's not fair." No doubt about it, before their consciences have been seared by the culture, children recognize that there is objective truth and a moral law. The *reductio ad absurdum* (reducing to the absurd) approach works great with small children because they immediately spot the contradictions of a worldview that tells them, "Truthfully, there is no truth!"

Many people simply don't know how to spot an opposing worldview, because on the surface it sounds so good. Consider some of the mass "inspirational" e-mails that seem to find their way into our inboxes. If there's flowery language and the word *God* in it, people (even professing Christians) think it must be good! I sometimes refer to these e-mailed items in my talks. When I analyze the content point by point, the audience picks up the errors immediately. An important question to ask small children regarding the postmodern worldview is, "Does that make sense?" Children often intuitively know it doesn't.

Here are several suggestions you can use to train the parents in your church to teach apologetics to children:

- Add quality resources to your book-lending library. Perhaps your congregation will commit to purchasing or donating a book on apologetics from a list you can provide. Take advantage of the wealth of apologetic resources available to the Christian community.[2] One of my favorite children's books, which I highly recommend to parents everywhere (and it's useful for Sunday school classes as well), is Dottie and Josh McDowell's *The Topsy-Turvy Kingdom*.[3] This delightful, beautifully illustrated book provides a wonderful springboard for discussion with small children.

- Enhance your media-lending library with lectures by popular apologists and especially debates. While doing housework, making dinner, or commuting to work, parents have an opportunity to equip themselves by listening to tapes or CDs—and guess who will be listening along with them? These days, of course, many families live "over the river and through the woods," and spend hours in their cars each week carpooling children to and fro. When I'm driving with my daughter, I'll often play an audiotape—sometimes stopping the tape to talk about what we've heard. One of our favorites is a debate between the late Dr. Walter Martin and Dr. Dale Miller.[4] I love to listen to Dr. Martin's lectures because I can feel his passion. He had a great sense of humor, spoke on a wide variety of topics, and had the incredible ability to break down heady concepts and put them into plain language. My daughter now asks me to play particular lectures of certain apologists or Bible teachers. *The Case for Christ*[5] on audiotape is one of her top ten favorites. While she may not understand everything she hears, seeds are being planted, and each time she grasps a little more.

- Remind the parents in your church that not only are our children watching our reaction to the cult member on our doorstep, but they're also watching us during worship, prayer, and the reading of the Word. Our reverence for God, like everything else, is contagious. The passion you exhibit for your Lord is the spark that can ignite the fire in your fellowship.

- Take seriously the Spirit of God dwelling in the children of your flock, no matter how young they are, and encourage their parents to do the same. Jesus said, "Let the little children come to me, and do not hinder them, for the kingdom of heaven belongs to such as these" (Matthew 19:14). Hindrance can take place when we brush off their questions or when we don't take their questions seriously. Nothing is more frustrating to a child.

- Encourage parents to know God's Word. It may sound simplistic, but what struck me as a new believer, and still does, is just how many professing Christians are biblically illiterate. Many have never read their Bibles from cover to cover, or they dismiss the Old Testament altogether, and as a result they don't really know God. Church leaders can be models by preaching and teaching the whole counsel of God. Also, encourage parents to engage in inductive Bible studies, whether through your church or such groups as Community Bible Study, Bible Study Fellowship, or Precept Ministries.[6] In many cases participants will also learn how to use study tools that will aid them in the area of apologetics.

- Invite speakers to your church who have the ability to put the cookies on the bottom shelf and make them not only fat free but edible. This should include not only male apologists but also women who can teach apologetics to the women in your fellowship in an engaging manner.[7]

IT'S ELEMENTARY

I really like J. P. Moreland's brass-tacks definition of apologetics: "Apologetics is a ministry designed to help unbelievers to overcome intellectual obstacles to conversion and believers to remove doubts that hinder spiritual growth."[8] My desire as a parent is that our children would not believe Christianity because my husband and I are Christians, or because we say it is true, or even because the learned apologists, pastors, or church leaders say it is true, but because they know it evidentially, experientially, and intellectually for themselves. Supplying our children with answers to questions when and even before they ask them, or before they are challenged by an unbeliever, will serve them well in seeing this desire come to fruition.

If you are a church leader or pastor, you have a wonderful opportunity to help parents fulfill the Great Commission in the lives of their children by passing on the torch that bears the Light of the world. You have a precious opportunity to watch the fruit of Deuteronomy 6 grow into effective witnesses for Jesus Christ as you heed his gracious words and "let your light shine before men, that they may see your good deeds and praise your Father in heaven" (Matthew 5:16).

QUESTIONS FOR REFLECTION AND DISCUSSION

1. In what ways are we helping our children examine the influences in their lives and how are we protecting their thought-lives? How are we doing in helping them discern truth from falsehood and in responding to their difficult questions?

2. Are our ministries to parents balanced, encouraging them to minister to people both inside and outside the church? Are the parents in our churches involved in reaching out to others in the natural relationships they form in their day-to-day experiences? How can we encourage them to do so?

3. Do the parents in our churches know why they believe what they believe? Can they defend their faith articulately? If not, how can we as leaders help them?

4. Are there mature parents in the faith who could begin an apologetics ministry for young parents within our fellowship?

Chapter 7

Off to College: Can We Keep Them?

J. Budziszewski

COLLEGE IS WAR

Christian college teachers who are "out of the closet" about their faith are sought out by Christian students who are wandering the wasteland of the modern campus in search of water. "In lecture today you mentioned that you're a Christian," said one young woman to me after class. "I've never heard that from any other professor, and every day I spend at this university I feel my faith is under attack."

I am as far out of the closet as a Christian teacher can be, in that my academic subject raises faith issues,[1] I write a monthly column in an online magazine for Christian students,[2] I speak on other campuses, and I've written a book about "how to stay Christian in college."[3] For this reason I get not only the usual office visits but also a good deal of mail from struggling college Christians. From that and from the apostasy of my own college years, I've developed a pretty good idea of how their faith gets in trouble.

Pastors and even parents often assume that the war against the faith is waged only in secular schools, so if our young people go to Christian colleges and universities, their life with Christ will be nourished instead of assaulted. This assumption is not merely false, but reckless. To be sure, there are some fine Christian schools. But the worst stories about anti-Christian ideological assault I have heard so far come from nominally Christian colleges that have not remained faithful to their mission. At one denominational college a Bible teacher is said to have begun each semester by hurling a Bible through the window and informing the students that by the end of the course none of them would still consider it the Word of God. He usually had his way.

Let's briefly consider the deficiencies in preparation that make Christian collegians vulnerable to assault. Afterward, and at greater length, I'll take up how pastors and church leaders can correct these deficiencies.

TWELVE REASONS WHY COLLEGIANS LOSE THEIR FAITH

Of course there are more than twelve reasons why so many college Christians lose their faith, but twelve is a nice round number that enables me to cover most of the territory economically.

A number of these dozen have to do with sex. That's not a reflection of my own obsessions but of the state of the struggle on campuses today. Perhaps in another age the main tasks of apologetics will have to do with war, with sickness, or with work. In ours they have to do with sex.

Young Believers Think They Can Be Solitary Christians

Many young believers go off to college with what I call the "just you and me, God" view of the Christian life. Separated from their hometown congregation, they think they can worship, pray, study Scripture, and practice the Christian disciplines all by themselves without fellowship with other believers. That's like a soldier thinking he can stay alive and fight just as well when separated from his unit.

They Don't Get the "Big Story" of Revelation

Some of the collegians I meet can quote passages of Scripture to me all day, but knowing them by heart is different from understanding them. Their grasp of revelation ought to be like a novel, with every episode adding to the whole. Instead, it's like a briefcase stuffed with scribbled memoranda: "Meeting Monday," "Call Tom," "Pick up eggs." The proverb "Where there is no vision, the people perish" applies to college students as well.

They Don't Know the Reasons for God's Rules

This deficiency is especially acute with regard to the "hot button" sexual issues that rage on college campuses today. When they are attacked for their beliefs, it's not enough for young Christians to know *that* God commands abstinence outside of marriage, *that* he invented marriage for one man and one woman, *that* he wants marriages to be fruitful—they must be able to explain why. God's rules must be practiced with understanding of and reflection on what the ancient rabbis called "the reasons of the Law."

They Don't Know That behind Every Temptation Is a False Ideology

At college, where gaining knowledge is the name of the game, even temptations gain most of their punch from false ideologies. Take the slogan "Sex is just like everything else; in order to make wise choices about it, you have to experience it." That's more than a "line"; it's a false philosophy. It says that the only way to know anything for sure is personal experience and that the test of experience is how you feel.

They Haven't Learned to Recognize the Desires and Devices of Their Hearts

It's an odd thing about us human beings: Not many of us disbelieve in God and then begin to sin—rather, we get involved in some clinging sin or start wanting to fit in, and then we find excuses to disbelieve in God. For this reason, the best apologetics in the world cannot succeed unless students know how to unmask their own secret motives.

They Think Good Intentions Are Enough to Protect Them from Sin

Like so many of the other stumbling blocks, this one is most prominent in the area of sex. For example, a Christian boy and girl may have every intention of remaining chaste but spend every waking moment alone together. This is an impossible combination.

Their Understanding of Christian Virtues Is Too Sentimental

Young Christians often confuse friendship with God with a state of their feelings. "I know the Bible says we should avoid doing such and such, but I prayed about it and *felt* that it was all right." Anyone who thinks like this is a sitting duck for the adversary, having become fatally vulnerable to attacks that would otherwise be easy to repel.

They Think Faith and Knowledge Are Opposites

Too many college Christians think that when the author of Hebrews said that faith is the "evidence of things not seen" (Hebrews 11:1 KJV), he meant that faith is blind—that no reasons can be given for Christian belief. Because their campus adversaries *do* give reasons for *their* beliefs, they feel defenseless.

They Think Jesus Forbids Moral Judgment

Young Christians often are easy targets for the accusation of intolerance, not because they really are intolerant, but because they *think* they are. Just because they believe and try to follow what Jesus taught about right and wrong, they think they must be violating his instruction not to "judge" (Matthew 7:1).

They Are Too Easily Frightened into Playing Defense

Feeling numerically outnumbered by nonbelieving students and intellectually outgunned by nonbelieving professors, Christian students are always replying to their critics, never playing critic themselves.

They Don't Realize That Their Adversaries Have Faith Commitments Too

A single illustration will suffice. When a nonbelieving biology teacher sneers at the Christian belief of creation by saying that "science" accepts only naturalistic explanations, young Christians usually don't notice that the teacher also lives by faith. He accepts by faith that nature is all there is—and he is so insistent about his faith that he refuses to consider the evidence in nature of intelligent design.

They Don't Know How to Call a Bluff

Young Christians let nonbelieving teachers and classmates get away with saying all kinds of things that they couldn't possibly believe. Why? They don't *realize* that their teachers and classmates couldn't possibly believe these things. They don't know how to call a bluff, because they don't know how to recognize one.

WHAT THE STUDENTS IN CHURCHES NEED TO HEAR FROM CHURCH LEADERSHIP

Let's take a closer look at what is missing in the preparation of young Christians for the challenges of college life.

What They Need to Hear about Solitary Christianity

It isn't enough to urge young Christians to go to church. They've heard that already, and they've probably had Hebrews 10:25 quoted to them until they're blue in the face: "Let us not give up meeting together, as some are in the habit of doing." What they really need is the correction of their excessively individualistic ecclesiology.

Don't think these young Christians don't have an ecclesiology just because they've never heard the term! Every Christian has an ecclesiology—a view of what the church is and what it is for. Unfortunately, some of the phrases we use to explain the Christian life to young people convey to them a false ecclesiology. We say to them, for example, that to be a Christian is to have "a personal relationship" with Jesus Christ or to make "a personal commitment" to Jesus Christ. The intention of these phrases is good—it is true that Christianity is not just a set of beliefs but a relationship with the living Lord and Savior, and it is true that it requires not just a belief lodged in the head but a commitment of the will. Unfortunately, the term *personal* in these phrases gives young people the wrong idea. It produces in them the "just you and me, God" view of Christian life I mentioned earlier.

Scripture never describes our relationship with Jesus Christ as "just you and me." Its emphasis is not on the solitary believer but on the community of faith. We are the "body" of Christ (1 Corinthians 12:27), the "people" of God, the "nation" he has called to holiness (1 Peter 2:9); we are citizens of the commonwealth of heaven (Philippians 3:20), in which we must "carry each other's burdens" (Galatians 6:2). God has always acted through a community. It was not good for Adam to be alone, so God made Eve. Not only Noah but his family was saved. Abraham was called so that from him and Sarah might come a people more numerous than the stars of heaven. On the day of Pentecost, God founded the church. God has made us social beings, and his plan of redemption through Jesus Christ is also social.

Explain these things, then, to the younger members of your flock while they are still teens, and tell them that their true peer group is the fellowship of the saints, the household of God. There is no such thing as a solitary Christian, and if they go into the world alone, they will be swallowed.

What They Need to Hear about the "Big Story" of Revelation

There are two things about revelation that very few students under-stand, yet both are crucial to their ability to defend their faith on the modern college campus. The first is the *reasonableness* of revelation; the second is its *plot*.

Revelation's Reasonableness

To many people of college age it seems unreasonable that God should have spoken to man—too magical, too weird. Yet, as we read in Isaiah, "my thoughts are not your thoughts, neither are your ways my ways, says the LORD. For as the heavens are higher than the earth, so are my ways higher than your ways and my thoughts than your thoughts" (Isaiah 55:8–9 RSV). John R. W. Stott makes this observation about this passage:

> It is ludicrous to suppose that we could ever penetrate into the mind of God. There is no ladder by which our little minds can climb up into His infinite mind. There is no bridge that we can throw across the chasm of infinity. There is no way to reach or to fathom God. . . . It is only reasonable to say . . . that unless God takes the initiative to disclose what is in His mind, we will never be able to find out."[4]

This is "the reasonableness of revelation."

Revelation's Plot

Although young Christians know "Bible stories," they often fail to realize that the Bible as a whole is a single great story—the *true* story, with extensive commentary, of God's dealings with humankind. College-age Christians need to hear from you that, like any story, the Bible contains characters, conflict, development, a turning point, a resolution, and an end. In this way they'll become equipped to see it as a whole.

Who are the characters? God, the people who come to know him, and the people who persist in rejecting him. What is the con-flict? That although God designed us for fellowship with him, we have rebelled against him beyond our power of returning and have broken ourselves beyond our power of repair. What is the development? That time after time he reaches out to us, that time after time we rebel again, but that he promises us a Rescuer who will be able to change our hearts. What is the turning point? That he visits us himself as a man of flesh and blood, accepting a criminal's death on the cross in order to take the burden of our rebellion and brokenness upon himself. What is the resolution? That by trusting this God-man as our sin bearer, we may be forgiven and begin to be transformed. And what is the end? That one day in heaven, the community of his people will be perfectly and permanently united with him, as a bride is united with her husband.

This story is the basis of all stories, the one and only context in which our own lives and struggles can make sense. Through sin we have tried to write ourselves out of God's story; through Jesus we can be written back in by him. This is what young Christians need to hear.

What They Need to Hear about the Reasons for God's Rules

A young person who is wondering whether the rules really come from God needs more than Scripture texts. He isn't asking, "Does the Bible teach this rule?" but "Why is this rule good?" In our age the question doesn't often arise about robbery (except by government), torture (except by abortion), or forsaking idols (except the self). It does arise about sex. Paradoxically, to understand the prohibitions regarding sex one has to understand why sex is *good,* and this is something most Christian students have never heard. Christianity takes a higher view of sex than any other religion. It's why it also has the strictest rules about it. Anything so important has to be handled carefully.

How can you explain this to younger Christians?[5] They need to learn that the first good is *procreation,* which means more than making babies. It also means raising children in the love and fear of God. You can make them without a marital commitment, but you can't raise them that way. The commitment must also be permanent, because the knowledge that your procreative partnership will continue into the then and there affects its quality in the here and now. Besides, once grown, the kids will have kids, and the kids' kids will need their parents' parents too. This is a matter of shattering importance. Every child is an image of God who will one day be older than the stars are today.

College-age Christians need to learn that the second great good is *union*. In marriage, sexual union takes each spouse out of the self for the sake of the other. Solitary sex can't achieve this; it keeps you locked in self. Homosexual sex can't achieve this; it directs you, narcissistically, to a mirror image of your self. Neither can casual sex achieve this; it endlessly joins and severs, joins and severs. Imagine what it would be like to repeatedly tear off and reattach your arm. There would come a day when no earthly surgery would suffice; the unitive power of your body would be lost. It is the same if you repeatedly tear off and reattach your various sexual partners. Eventually they all seem like strangers, and you just don't feel anything. You have destroyed your capacity for intimacy.

And teach them that the third great good is *mystery*. This good is realized only when the spouses belong to Christ, for they become a *living emblem* of his sacrificial love for the church and of the church's adoring response. Paul is so awed that he calls matrimony one of God's secrets: "This is a profound mystery—but I am talking about Christ and the church" (Ephesians 5:32). The little humilities and the mutual sacrifices of the husband and wife are a training for the heavenly union between Christ and his church; the awe of their wedding night and the ecstasy of their embraces, a parable of it.

What They Need to Hear about the False Ideologies Lurking behind Temptations

There are two ways to armor young Christians against ideological seduction. The first way is to anticipate and answer the ideologies they are most likely to meet. For example, I commented earlier that the slogan "Sex is just like everything else; in order to make wise choices about it, you have to experience it" expresses a philosophy of knowledge. Once they spot this philosophy, you can put it in the witness box and start cross-examining it. Is it really true that the only way to know anything for sure is personal experience? Are there any cases where personal experience works *against* knowledge? (How about suicide and drug addiction?) And is it really true that the test of experience is how you feel? Haven't you ever felt good about something that turned out to be bad?

You will never be able to anticipate and answer every single ideological seduction, so an even better way to armor young Christians is to teach them to spot them on their own. To give them practice, throw them "lines." After each line ask, "What philosophy lies behind this line?" Let them conduct the cross-examination on their own. Encourage them to develop discernment, that spiritual and intellectual sense of smell that tells them "something is rotten here."

What They Need to Hear about the Desires and Devices of Their Hearts

Jeremiah remarks, "The heart is deceitful above all things and beyond cure. Who can understand it?" (Jeremiah 17:9). Unfortunately, this is also true of Christians. Our old fallen nature continues to compete with the Christ-life that is taking shape in us; we may "put to death" our fallen nature, as Paul exhorts (Romans 8:13; Colossians 3:5), but even then it twitches with galvanic life. Until heaven, when our sanctification is complete, we will be prone to self-deception.

A young woman once asked me for a letter of recommendation to a theological seminary. I asked her why she wanted to enter seminary. She told me she was desperate to hold on to her faith but drowning in unanswered questions; she hoped that in seminary she would find the answers. Yet when I glanced at her application form, I found that she had chosen perhaps the most way-out seminary in the country, a den of disbelief. Through conversation I learned that in her last year of university she had avoided taking courses from believing professors (who were rare enough in any case), instead seeking professors notorious for their enmity to faith. Moreover, when I asked her what her unanswered questions were, they turned out to be fairly simple.

"I think you are mistaken about your motives for going to seminary," I told her. "You're behaving not like someone who wants answers but like someone who wants to avoid them. Could it be that you're *seeking* reasons to lose your faith—that you're manufacturing a dramatic crisis—so that you can lose your faith and say afterward, 'I couldn't help it'?"

My experience is that no college student loses her faith unless at some level she wants to; the slip lies not in the intellect but in the will. This may imply that it's easy to hold on to faith. Not so: The difficulty lies in recognizing what we really want, because we really do not want to recognize it. College students need to learn that we sinners cannot fully trust our own perceptions; all of us must pray as David did:

> Who can discern his errors?
> > Forgive my hidden faults.
> Keep your servant also from willful sins;
> > may they not rule over me.
> Then will I be blameless,
> > innocent of great transgression.
>
> *Psalm 19:12–13*

What They Need to Hear about the Limits of Good Intentions

I've already explained one limit of good intentions—they may not be as good as we think. Even when they really are good, however, they are not enough.

By way of example, I mentioned earlier the absurdity of a Christian boy and girl having every intention of remaining chaste but spending every waking moment alone together. The problem here is not just that they have no sense of their own weaknesses (which is pride), but that in a sense, they are setting themselves against God's design for human sexuality (which is presumption). Being alone with the beloved is *supposed* to be arousing; that's how God made us. Aloneness is what one seeks with one's spouse; it is a precursor to intercourse. To be alone with the beloved but trying not to be aroused is like turning on a powerful rocket motor and saying "Don't lift off."

What usually happens next is that the boy and girl try to deal with the resulting temptations by praying together about them. I can't think of a faster way to wind up in bed, for now they are combining the sexual drive with the spiritual drive, and their rocket has shifted from chemical propulsion to warp drive.[6] By now, of course, their good intentions *have* turned bad, because they have committed a particularly attractive sin and may find it difficult to repent. It's at this time that faith begins to seem "unreal," and the best apologetics in the world may do no good.

This cautionary tale shows why even knowing the reasons for God's rules is not enough (see pages 110–11). Colleges students also need a generous dose of godly common sense—what God in the book of Proverbs calls wisdom.

What They Need to Hear to Avoid Sentimental Misunderstandings of Christian Virtue

My generation bears most of the blame for sentimentalizing Christianity. "When I read in Mark how Jesus cursed the fig tree, I *feel* much closer to him," said one woman in a Bible study group. "Jesus is a sinner, just like me!" No argument could convince her that she had drastically misinterpreted the passage. "Feelings are neither right nor wrong," runs the misleading mantra, "they just are."

Among college students, sentimentalism has run amuck. Consider faith, for instance. Because young Christians confuse faith with warm feelings toward God, when their feelings are running cool, they think they must be having a crisis of faith. Soon it becomes a real crisis of faith; like those who refuse to believe what they cannot see, they refuse to believe what they cannot feel.

Or consider hope. Because young Christians confuse hope with feelings of optimism, when they hear theories that presume that humans can somehow fix their problems and "save themselves," they think they should go along. Hope then becomes complacency about the course of this present broken world—or a utopian idolatry of the "human spirit."

Consider finally the greatest spiritual virtue, namely, love. Because young Christians confuse love with trying to enter into their neighbors' feelings, when people who espouse disordered ways of life express feelings of pain and anger, they "feel" they ought to take their side. It may never occur to them that the pain might be self-inflicted, or that the anger might be a way to avoid the real issue. This helps explain why the gay rights movement can be such a source of anguish for young Christians.

What the younger members of your congregation need to hear is that the spiritual virtues are not feelings but deep-seated dispositions of the mind and will. Faith means continuing to believe and trust the promises of God, even when the feelings of trust have faltered; God uses the cool seasons of our feelings to exercise us, like a muscle. Hope means fixing our eyes on heaven even when the feelings of confidence have waned; now we see as in a mirror, darkly, but then we shall see face to face (see I Corinthians 13:12). Love means acting for the true good of other persons, even when their hearts desire what poisons their souls and they can only hear the words of love as hate.

Sentiment is shifting sand. You can have warm feelings toward God without faith, you can have feelings of optimism without hope, and you can have feelings of sympathy without love. Our God is not sand; he's a Rock.

What They Need to Hear about the Relation between Faith and Knowledge

If secular college teachers mention faith at all, they treat it as the opposite of knowledge; they think it means believing things without having any reasons. From this point of view it seems that faith hinders the search for truth; it gets in the way of reasoning. Too many of our college students assume this to be true.

People who say they rely not on faith but on reasoning alone haven't carefully considered what reasoning is. Reasoning itself depends on faith. How could this be? Easy. Suppose you tried to prove, not by faith but by reason alone, that reason works. You couldn't do it. The only way to show that reasoning works would be to reason about it. But in that case you'd be assuming ahead of time what you set out to prove— the reliability of reason. Circular arguments prove nothing. How then do we know that reasoning works? We take it on trust. On faith.

This argument is not the same as saying that no good reasons can be given for reasoning. Many good reasons can be given for reasoning and for other important things as well. We should heed them. The point is that having good reasons does not remove the necessity of trust. Augustine understood this point well; he said, "I believe in order to know." If you don't believe something, you will never understand anything.

An example most students understand comes from relational knowledge. I *know* many things about my wife that I never could have learned unless I *trusted* her enough to make an irrevocable commitment to her—to enter into the relationship of matrimony. Matrimony, then, is a high-rolling faith commitment. To be sure, before I leaped I had good reasons to think there was solid ground on the other side. But I couldn't *see* it; not even a hundred good reasons could have made it other than a leap. Only by *trusting* her could I *know* that my trust had been justified.

Why leap at all? Why trust in anything? The option of not trusting is not available. To refuse to leap is to take on trust that you will be all right if you just remain where you are—and that, too, is a leap. The difference is not between leaping and not leaping, but between a leap that knows itself to be a leap and a leap that pretends it is not a leap.

What They Need to Hear about Moral Judgment

"How dare you *judge* my opinion?" "By expressing that belief you're *judging* me." "What hypocrites you Christians are. Jesus told you not to be *judgmental,* but you *judge* more than anyone does."

It is ridiculously easy to explode these fallacies. When Jesus said, "Do not judge," he didn't mean we were not to judge opinions as true or false (for he did that all the time), that we were not to judge behavior (he did that, too), or even that we were not to make judgments of character (remember what he said about the Pharisees). What he meant was that we are not to preempt God's final judgment at the end of history, when the saved will be separated from the damned; we are not to treat anyone as outside the circle of God's love. Paul puts the point in these words: "Therefore do not pronounce judgment before the time, before the Lord comes, who will bring to light the things now hidden in darkness and will disclose the purposes of the heart" (1 Corinthians 4:5 RSV). Jesus models it. His final words to the woman caught in adultery were "Neither do I condemn you. Go now and leave your life of sin" (John 8:11). He did not condemn her, yet he obviously "judged" that she had sinned.

If these fallacies are so easy to explode, then what gives them their grip on our young people? Have they never heard the distinction expressed in the slogan "Hate the sin but love the sinner"? They have. Then what is the problem? The problem is the false ideology of "identity politics," which refuses to allow the distinction between sin and sinner in the first place. Consider, for example, gay activists. They make their sexual feelings and behavior the very basis of who they are. If a young Christian says to an activist, "I'm not condemning you but loving you—I am trying to say that what you do is killing you," they reply, "Your love is meaningless. I am what I do. By judging what I do, you *are* condemning me."

To enable student believers to keep their heads in such confrontations, you must add two elements to their preparation. First, for the guarding of their understanding, they need to know that no human being has the liberty to make up his or her own identity. God has defined our identity already—and not just by words (though his words are power). He has given to every human being an identity by creation (see Genesis 1:26–27; 9:6), and he has given to each believer yet a deeper identity by redemption.[7] Second, for the guarding of their hearts, they need to distinguish their love for their neighbor from their understandable desire to have this love welcomed by the neighbor. There is never a guarantee that true love will be recognized as true love by the beloved (see Matthew 5:11–12). We must please God, not people (see Galatians 1:10; 1 Thessalonians 2:4).

What They Need to Hear about Offense and Defense

It's true that college Christians are outnumbered by their nonbelieving classmates, but "if God is for us, who can be against us?" (Romans 8:31). When Christians have no need to fear violent persecution, as in this part of the world, some begin to expect the world to be a friend. Then they slip into seeking the world's approval instead of God's. When a classmate or coworker rolls his or her eyes, they go hollow.

The resistance strategy here is not to exhort young people to resist peer pressure; it can't be done, and it doesn't need to be done. It can't be, because all people care what their "reference group" thinks of them. It doesn't need to be, because peer pressure is good—if it's the right kind of pressure from the right kind of peers! Our reference group must be our brothers and sisters in Christ.

It's also true that college Christians are intellectually outgunned by their nonbelieving professors. If they already knew everything their professors knew and had developed all the skills their professors had developed, they wouldn't be in school. But they have two great advantages, the importance of which they hardly recognize. One is that the presuppositions that underlie the anti-Christian worldviews of their professors aren't true; they do not correspond to reality. The other is that their adversaries are self-deceived. The defense of deep untruth is so difficult that defenders are driven time and time again to say things so preposterous that even they cannot really believe them. The key is to *call their bluff.*

Just how young Davids can take on such Goliaths will be explored in the next two sections. Above all, however, they need to be reminded that the best defense of faith—make that the *only* defense of faith—is a good (though humble) offense. One way for pastors and church leaders to get this point across is to have their collegians list the items that Paul includes in the "armor of God" (Ephesians 6:10–18):

the belt of truth
the breastplate of righteousness
the footguards of readiness to spread the gospel
the shield of faith
the helmet of salvation
the sword of the Spirit, which is the word of God
and prayer (which seems to lace the rest together)

Now ask them this question: What part of the body is left unprotected? Answer: No armor is mentioned for the back. All of it is for the front.

The meaning is obvious. God does not intend his people ever to turn their backs to the adversary. He intends us to advance when we can and stand when we must but to never retreat.

The same point is made in John Bunyan's classic allegory *The Pilgrim's Progress,* when Christian, the hero of the story, meets a foe far stronger than himself.

> But now in this Valley of Humiliation poor Christian was hard put to it; for he had gone but a little way before he espied a foul fiend coming over the field to meet him; his name is Apollyon. Then did Christian begin to be afraid, and to cast in his mind whether to go back or to stand his ground. But he considered again that he had no armour for his back; and therefore thought that to turn the back to him might give him the greater advantage with ease to pierce him with his darts. Therefore he resolved to venture and stand his ground; for, thought he, had I no more in mine eye than the saving of my life, it would be the best way to stand.[8]

What They Need to Hear about the Faith Commitments of Their Adversaries

No one has the option of not having faith; the only real issue is whether to have faith in *this* or in *that*. Therefore, when young Christians hear from their teachers or classmates that faith has no place in the life of the mind, pastors should remind them of the faith commitments of those who say these things.

In the humanities, for example, many of their teachers will be postmodernists. Postmodernists pride themselves on their "suspicion of metanarratives," their conviction that no one gets the Big Story right (the story about who we are, where we came from, why we are here, and so forth). Of course, postmodernists always make a tacit exception for their *own* Big Story, the story that no one gets the Big Story right. What they really mean, then, is that *no one else* gets the Big Story right. How can they justify the exception? If no one else gets the Big Story right, how can they get it right? The answer is that they don't justify the exception; rarely do they even admit to it. The tacit exception rests on a tacit faith that all people are boobs but themselves. In fact, this is just the kind of faith they mock, because they cannot give a reason for it. That's why the exception is tacit.

The faith commitment of postmodernists is not particularly difficult for students to spot. Many students do spot it. But they think, "This can't be right. It's just too silly. There must be more to postmodernism than this. I must have misunderstood the teacher." No, they understood the teacher perfectly. It *is* too silly.

In the sciences we more often find a different faith commitment, namely, the conviction that nature—material nature—is all there is. Christians would call this a belief in creation without a creator. Philosophers call it naturalism, or materialism. Confronted with the mounting scientific evidence of intelligent design,[9] naturalists do not reply with counterevidence; they simply rule the evidence out of order. It cannot count as evidence, they say, because science considers only naturalistic explanations. Did you think that science was following the evidence wherever it might lead? How silly of you, they think. As Richard Lewontin of Harvard has written:

> Our willingness to accept scientific claims that are against common sense is the key to an understanding of the real struggle between science and the supernatural. We take the side of science *in spite* of the patent absurdity of some of its constructs, *in spite* of its failure to fulfill many of its extravagant promises of health and life, *in spite* of the tolerance of the scientific community for unsubstantiated just-so stories, because we have a prior commitment, a commitment to materialism. It is not that the methods and institutions of science somehow compel us to accept a material explanation of the phenomenal world, but, on the contrary, that we are forced by our *a priori* adherence to material causes to create an apparatus of investigation and a set of concepts that produce material explanations, no matter how counterintuitive, no matter how mystifying to the uninitiated. Moreover, that materialism is absolute, for we cannot allow a Divine Foot in the door.[10]

This is quite an impressive list of "in spite ofs." The naturalistic faith commitment is just as easy to spot as the postmodernist faith commitment and just as unreasonable: You cannot give a reason for something if its only foundation is refusing to consider all the evidence. Not all faith is blind, but naturalistic faith is blind—blind hostility to the possibility of God.

What They Need to Hear about Calling Bluffs

Every successful calling of an intellectual bluff has two parts—an unmasking and a follow-through. Here's an example. The bluffer says, "Morality is all relative anyway. How do we even know that murder is wrong?" You ask, "Are you at this moment in any actual doubt about murder being wrong?" He replies, "Well, no." Now that you've unmasked him, you say, "Good. Then let's talk about something you really are in doubt about." That's the follow-through.

Here's another. The bluffer says, "Nobody knows any truth." You reply, "If you really believed that, you wouldn't say it." He replies, "Why not?" You answer, "Because then you wouldn't know if it was true!" Now that you've unmasked him, you follow through. "So let me ask you: What do you get out of *pretending* to think that nobody knows any truth?"

Sometimes the unmasking and the follow-through can be combined. For instance, the bluffer might say, "Okay, so you caught me saying something that has no meaning. So what? I don't need truth, and I don't need meaning." You reply, "I don't believe you, because we both know that the longing for truth and meaning is deeply set in every intellect, yours as well as mine. The real question, then, is this: What are you so desperate to have that you're willing to give up even meaning to get it?"

Young Christians rarely succeed in calling their adversaries' bluffs. Anyone may miss an opportunity, but the problem lies deeper than this, namely, they don't know how. The reason they don't know how to call a bluff is that they don't know how to spot one in the first place. To spot it, they would have to know that the bluffer was saying something he or she couldn't really mean. To do that (unless they were mind readers), they would have to know that there are certain things that everyone really knows. With rare exceptions, college-age Christians don't know that there are certain things that everyone really knows. You need to tell them.

The theological term for "what everyone really knows" is *general revelation*. General revelation is what God has revealed not directly, through the Bible, but indirectly, apart from it. This is not an antibiblical doctrine; the Bible itself says that God has not left himself without a witness among the nonbelievers. In fact, he has left himself at least six witnesses among them, and young Christians need to learn how to appeal to each one of them.[11]

The witness of *conscience* is "written on the heart" (Romans 2:15), and although it can be suppressed (see Romans 1:18), it can never be erased. The witness of *Godward longing* whispers to every person that his or her idols can never save but that there is an Unknown God who can (see Acts 17:22–32). The witness of God's *handiwork* proclaims the glory of the Creator through his creation—not only in the heavens (see Psalm 19:1–6; 104; Acts 14:17; Romans 1:20), but in his images, namely, ourselves (see Genesis 1:26–27; 9:6; Psalm 139:13–14). The witness of the *harvest* is that every sin is linked with consequences; whatever we sow, we reap (see Proverbs 1:31; Jeremiah 17:10; Hosea 10:12; Galatians 6:7). The witness of *practical order* emerges from our observations and labors in the natural world God has made. For example, a wise farmer knows that certain ways of doing things cooperate with the natural order, while others "go against the grain" and fail (see Isaiah 28:23–29). Finally, the witness of our *design* is the witness of practical order applied to ourselves, for some of God's intentions are reflected in the "blueprint" of our physical, intellectual, and emotional nature—either in the general nature men and women share or in the special nature he has given each.[12] These matters bear long reflection.

General revelation is paradoxical because on the one hand nonbelievers know it, but on the other they try to convince themselves that they don't know it. They are self-deceived. By understanding what the Bible teaches about general revelation, we achieve a strategic advantage: *We* know what they know better than *they* know what they know. That's why even a college-age Christian can learn to call their bluffs.

THEN CAN WE KEEP THEM?

They are off to college. Can we keep them? Yes! Loyalty to Jesus Christ is attacked in every time and in every land; it is not for nothing that the early church fathers spoke of the church militant. Yet God has carried his people through every tribulation, and the gates of hell have not prevailed.

Just as the art of physical battle changes from age to age, so does the art of spiritual battle. We are going through another transformation. Infantry are no match for iron chariots, nor iron chariots for jet planes. In the same way, the apologetical weapons and catechetical armor that served young Christians during the Enlightenment must be reforged to meet the challenges of postmodernity. Their pastors and church leaders must show them how to use these tools.

It is probably true that pastors today must be more self-conscious about these matters than in former days. It was once believed that the culture was Christian. Today the nominal church itself is a mission field. Pastors in their own countries and congregations must often be like ambassadors to strange lands.

Yet was the culture ever really Christian? Perhaps not. Perhaps in former days its assaults and temptations were merely harder to recognize because they *sounded* Christian. Today, by contrast, they are obvious. That's not bad; an attack that can be seen can be more easily repelled.

We *can* keep our college-age people. Not by our wit but by the grace of God we can keep them. It was he who gave our young people their minds, and it is he who can transform them and claim them as his own. He kept a people for himself through wars and famines, through invasions and inundations, through exiles and persecutions. He kept their souls beneath the swords of their pagan emperors—and if only we serve him faithfully, he will keep our college students beneath the sneers of their teachers.

QUESTIONS FOR REFLECTION AND DISCUSSION

1. Why is it so important for Christian students to have a sound ecclesiology—a sound understanding of the nature of the church?

2. Why is it so important for Christian students to revise their understanding of the relation between faith and reason?

3. Why is it so important for Christian students to deepen their understanding of special revelation?

4. Why is it so important for Christian students to acquire an understanding of general revelation?

5. Why is it so important for Christian students to have godly common sense—what the Bible calls wisdom?

6. What does it mean to call a teacher's bluff? Can this be done with gentleness and respect, as the Bible requires in 1 Peter 3:15?

Chapter 8

Issues and Approaches in Working with Internationals

Dean C. Halverson

For most Americans, rubbing shoulders with people from other nations has become an everyday part of their lives. Such diversity is not surprising; according to the U.S. Census Bureau, in 1997 nearly one resident in ten was foreign born (25.8 million).[1] The United States is indeed living up to its reputation of being the melting pot of the nations.

To add to the diversity, there are more than 650,000 international students studying in U.S. colleges and universities, most of whom are here only temporarily as they earn their undergraduate or graduate degrees. When they complete their studies, a majority of them will return to their home countries to become voices of influence among their people.

When most Christians think of missions, they think overseas. But, through immigrants and international students, God has brought the overseas mission field to the very doorstep of the American church. God has given American Christians an amazing opportunity to reach the world for him without even having to travel beyond the borders of our own county—or community. It is one thing to know that there are internationals among us; it is quite another matter to know how to reach them with the gospel. How do we share the gospel with people who come from religious or worldview perspectives such as Hinduism, Buddhism, Islam, or atheism that are so drastically different from ours? This is where apologetics comes into play.

Practical apologetics should not be separated from evangelism but should instead be seen as a vital part of the evangelistic process. And when talking about sharing the gospel with internationals, evangelism must indeed be seen as a process, not as a onetime event.

Generally, the initial part of the evangelism process should have nothing to do with an intellectual defense of the gospel but should instead have everything to do with building a friendship. One of the most common criticisms that internationals lodge against Americans is that, while Americans come across as friendly initially, their friendship doesn't run very deep. In the original cultures of the internationals, friendship means more than having a passing acquaintance with a person; it means spending time with that person.

Building a friendship takes time and commitment. At times it might not be convenient, but it is nevertheless an essential part of the process of evangelizing the international. Through friendship building we are building a bridge of trust that will be able to carry the weight of truth.

Building a friendship means helping internationals become settled into their new surroundings. It means incorporating internationals into family activities. It also means not only asking about their lives—such as their family back in their country of origin, their culture, their holidays, their educational system, their religion, and their interests—but also sharing our lives with them. When conversing with internationals, we need to find a balance between asking them about their lives and sharing about ours. People share best when it is done in the context of a naturally flowing conversation in which both sides, not just one, share their thoughts and backgrounds.

As the friendship is being built, we need to allow the Holy Spirit to lead us as to when we should share our faith with our international friend in a sensitive and noncoercive manner. A natural way to guide the conversation toward spiritual matters is to ask our friend about religion in his or her country and then to ask about his or her beliefs. Don't assume that, just because people come from a Muslim or Hindu country, they buy the "party line" on every point. They probably will have some individualized opinions that differ from the standard teachings of their culture's religion.

One person who works with internationals made this pertinent observation:

> Asking questions is absolutely critical. Learning to ask questions has been the most liberating and effective strategy I've learned over the years. It takes the pressure off having to guess at the other's worldview, and it gives you an opportunity to identify conversational "points of entry." It also shows respect and value for the other's opinion. Also, I used to be—and most American Christians are—nervous about evangelism, precisely because I viewed it primarily in terms of "telling" rather than "asking." The power of a good question to stimulate the mind is immense.[2]

As your international friend is talking about his or her beliefs, listen for key words that reveal what the international is looking for in religion. He or she might be looking for forgiveness, guidance, meaning, fulfillment, a moral foundation, power to change morally, fellowship with God, or assurance as to what will happen after death. Then share your testimony. If you can share your testimony in a way that relates it to what your friend is looking for in religion, all the better, but don't force your testimony to conform to something that it's not. Or the international's words may reveal that he or she is looking for nothing more than the "American dream." We need to be patient with people enamored by materialism, as we wait for a point of crisis or a spirit of openness in their lives.[3]

Never underestimate the power of your life to communicate the gospel. As a Christian, you are the embodiment of Christ for your international friends. Your acts of kindness, such as taking a batch of cookies to them, will speak volumes. Also, ask for their permission to pray with and for them. As they see God work in their lives, they will be attracted to him. Above all, be sure that there are no strings attached to your friendship. Your friendships should not be contingent on your international friends accepting the Christian faith.

APOLOGETICS AS ATTRACTION

When dealing with a person who has a different religion or world-view, the tendency of many Christians is to prematurely answer questions the person hasn't yet asked. We anticipate that, since they are Muslim or Hindu or Buddhist, they will have certain objections to Christianity, so we often put those questions in their mouths prematurely. They may indeed have such questions, but, on the other hand, they may not. Let nonbelievers bring up their questions and objections; we don't need to. Our initial role should be to make the idea of getting to know God attractive. We as Christians should be so sold on the thrill of knowing God that the international will be attracted to such a relationship.

Stretch Their Thinking about God

Some internationals show a certain complacency concerning God. It's not so much that they don't believe in God as that knowing God or having a personal relationship with him is not a strong desire or need for them. It's simply not a high priority. For others, the prospect of having to face God in judgment is not a big deal. Sure, we have messed up, but many internationals believe that most people are basically good. Plus, since God is loving at the core, there really shouldn't be any problem when we face him. To believe otherwise, they say, is to portray God as intolerant and unloving. And then there are the atheists-evolutionists who believe that when we die, we simply cease to exist, and that's all there is to it. In the face of such attitudes, sometimes it's best to shock people, to shake them out of their comfortable thinking about God and the prospect of standing before him.

One place you can find common ground for beginning such a discussion is in the book *Contact* by scientist-atheist Carl Sagan. In that book, Sagan has Ellie, the main character, making this statement:

> The theologians seemed to have recognized a special nonrational—I wouldn't call it irrational—aspect of the feeling of sacred or holy. They call it "numinous." The term was first used by ... let's see ... somebody named Rudolph Otto in a 1923 book, *The Idea of*

the Holy. He believed that humans were predisposed to detect and revere the numinous. He called it *misterium tremendum. . . .*

In the presence of the *misterium tremendum,* people feel utterly insignificant but, if I read this right, not personally alienated. He thought of the numinous as a thing "wholly other," and the human response to it as "absolute astonishment." Now, if that's what religious people talk about when they use words like sacred or holy, I'm with them.[4]

"Utterly insignificant," "wholly other," "absolute astonishment"—Ellie says that if this is what religious people mean when talking about experiencing the sacred or the holy, then she's with them. And this is precisely the kind of God we encounter in the Bible. For example, God said to Moses in Exodus 33:20, "You cannot see my face, for no one may see me and live." And Paul described God as the one who "lives in unapproachable light, whom no one has seen or can see" (1 Timothy 6:16). A God who says "no one may see me and live" and who "lives in unapproachable light" is indeed "wholly other" and would fill us with "absolute astonishment."

But we must also understand that, while such a God is certainly the sacred for which we long, he is not safe. We do not have the automatic right to stand in his presence. The idea that we as finite beings are able to stand in the presence of the infinite God—the one who has existence within himself—is as unlikely as our being able to stand five feet away from the sun without being incinerated.

Paradoxically, though, such a God is exactly the kind of being who will fulfill us. How can this be? Because only this kind of God is worthy of our getting to know him for an eternity. We will never plumb the depths of such an infinitely awesome God. If we settle for anything less in God, we are settling for less in ourselves as well, for we can never rise above the nature of what we consider to be ultimate reality. If, for example, we say that ultimate reality is nothing more than matter, which is what atheists contend, then the logical implication is that we ourselves are nothing more than mere matter. Or if we say that ultimate reality is an impersonal oneness that is beyond all distinctions, which is what many Hindus believe, then our existence as persons loses its value. But if God is infinite in his being and personhood, our desire for knowing him can never be entirely satiated. Listen to the wise words of one international: "If God were small enough for us to fully understand him, he wouldn't be big enough for us to worship."[5] Again, we as Christians need to be so sold on getting to know God that the international will be attracted to getting to know him as well.

The Hope within You

The apostle Peter wrote, "Always be prepared to give an answer to everyone who asks you to give the reason for the hope that you have" (1 Peter 3:15). As Peter's words reveal, there is a place for giving reasoned answers to the questions and objections of the unbeliever. And many Christian apologists are almost exclusively focused on such an intellectual approach. However, we must not fail to see—and thereby to live—the end to which such answers point, namely, "the hope that we have." Living a life of hope based on the truths of the gospel can speak volumes to the international. Bill Mitchell, a staff member with International Students, Inc., writes, "I am becoming increasingly convinced that it is 'the hope' that we have that causes students to look deeper at our reasons. Are we people who exemplify hope in our daily lives?"[6]

The Good News/Bad News Principle

Another attractive theme in the Christian message is the good news of Jesus Christ, but it must be placed in the context of the bad news. One of the teachings that sets Christianity apart from other world religions and worldviews is the severity of humanity's spiritual problem. The Christian gospel begins not just with bad news, but with terribly bad news. The bad news could not be worse. Humanity is not just hurting spiritually, we are spiritually dead (see Romans 5:6, 8; 6:23; Ephesians 2:1).

Other religions say humans are spiritually bad off but fixable, and we're fixable through our own power. The Hindu would say that our primary problem is that we have forgotten who we are in our true divine selves, and that through various spiritual techniques we can regain that enlightened consciousness. The Buddhist would say that our primary problem is that of being attached to that which is impermanent, which causes us to suffer, but we can fix it by ceasing to desire. The Muslim would say that our primary problem is that we don't follow God's laws, but we can fix this by striving to follow God's laws. The secularist would say that our primary problem is that we don't act rationally, and all we need to do is get rid of religious superstition and determine to see everything from a rational perspective.

In Christianity, however, we humans do not have the power within us to fix ourselves. We have sinned, and "the wages of sin is death" (Romans 6:23a). Our situation is as bad off as that of the drowning man in the middle of the huge lake who, as he goes down for the third time, yells, "Self-help, self-help!" That's the bad news. The good news is that the Christian gospel ends with tremendously good news: "but the gift of God is eternal life in Christ Jesus our Lord" (verse 23b).

Christianity, then, begins with bad news and ends with good news. The other world religions, on the other hand, begin with what appears to be good news, but they end with bad news. One of the things the Christian needs to listen for when talking with someone from a non-Christian religion or worldview is the way in which that person may begin with a teaching that sounds like good news. For example, someone may say, "God is unconditionally loving toward all. He will not judge anyone." Or someone else may say, "I believe that there are as many paths to God as there are paths to the top of a mountain." But there is bad news that lurks behind such statements.

Consider the first statement: "God is unconditionally loving toward all. He will not judge anyone." In other words, God will accept all people into his presence. While such a statement is certainly in tune with today's spirit of tolerance, would a God who is unconditionally loving indeed accept all people into his presence, no matter what their actions were on earth? Are there no moral standards to God's love? And how does such love relate to the idea that God is holy? Consider the logical implications of the idea that God will accept everyone and judge no one:

- If God allows everyone into his kingdom just the way they are morally, then it means he must allow mass murderers, such as Hitler, Stalin, and Pol Pot, and serial killers into his kingdom. Would God's kingdom still be heaven, or would it be hell?

- If God allows everyone into his kingdom just the way they are morally, then it means he has condoned their actions. Would not such acceptance reflect flaws in God's character? Would we want to associate with such a God? Could we trust such a God? Would this be heaven, or hell?
- If God is absolutely holy and yet all people are ushered into his presence without any moral change having been effected in their hearts, might it not be a greater punishment for sinners to be in the presence of an absolutely holy God than what hell would be?
- If God allows all people into his kingdom, but only after he has changed them to make them loving people—regardless of whether or not they wanted to be changed—then did he not make them into robots with no free will? Would not the value of our personhood have been diminished?[7]

Such implications are the bad news that follows the apparent good news that God loves all and will judge none.

We as Christians believe that God does love us unconditionally (the good news) but only because he paid the heavy price—death—for the consequences of our sinful actions (the bad news). God's unconditional love is based on the condition that the penalty for our sin was paid on our behalf through the substitutionary death of Jesus Christ.

Consider next the statement: "There are as many paths to God as there are paths to the top of a mountain." The good news in such a thought is that no one will be judged for failing to choose the right path to God, because there is no wrong path. We each can choose whichever path suits us best.

But again there is bad news that lurks behind such a statement. The bad news is to be found in the emphasis in the analogy—in the path *we* must walk. In other words, salvation in such a view is a gradual process based on human effort. Also, the bad news is that we can have no assurance concerning what happens after death, because we will never be certain that we have met the required standard.

The true good news is that salvation, according to Christianity, is a gift to be received, not something to be earned through human effort.

Moreover, because God has accomplished salvation on our behalf and we merely receive it, we can have the full assurance that nothing can take this salvation away from us (see Romans 8:38–39).

Approach Them on the Level of Their Emotions and Imagination

Another way to attract internationals to the gospel is by touching them on the emotional level and on the level of their imagination. Because we are multileveled creatures made in the image of God, the intellectual level shouldn't be our only avenue of approach. "People need facts to know what decision to make," wrote one evangelist, "but emotion to get them to make the decision."[8] And the way to touch people on the emotional level is through an image or word picture, such as a testimony, a story, or an illustration. For example, be aware of the movies the internationals are watching and the books they're reading, and be willing to discuss them. Some movies and books have great analogies to the gospel. For example, while I wouldn't agree with everything taught in the movie *What Dreams May Come,* I did see some similarities between Christy and Annie's plight and the gospel message (which I mentioned to an international student friend). Some of the similarities include the following:

- The name of Annie's husband is "Christy." I don't think the similarity between Christy and Christ is coincidental, considering Christy's actions are very much like those of Christ.
- Just as love was Christy's motivation for saving his wife from hell, so love was also God's motivation for sending his Son to earth to save us.
- The turning point for Annie's release from her prison in hell was Christy's decision to join her and stay with her in hell rather than to return to heaven—precisely what Jesus Christ had to do to win our release from sin and hell as well. He whose dwelling was heaven became one of us on earth.
- Annie could not save herself. She didn't have anything even approaching the power necessary to release herself from the

prison of hell. It took someone who would come from outside of hell to save her. In the same way, we cannot save ourselves.

• Just as the movie climaxed with the reuniting of Christy and Annie and then with their children, so is our fulfillment—both in this life and in the afterlife—to be found in relationships, particularly in our relationship with God.

The movie made it clear that hell is indeed a terrible place and that heaven is a wonderful place—truths with which the Bible would very much agree.

KEEP GOD'S PERSONHOOD IN MIND

Probably the single most basic truth that sets Christianity apart from the other world religions is that *God is a personal being.* While one would not think that such a basic truth would be unique among the world religions, in fact, many of them actually push God away rather than make him known. They make God out to be distant, abstract, unknowable, and even inconceivable. For example, the ultimate idea for God in Hinduism is called *nirguna Brahman. Nirguna* means "without attributes." Something that has no attributes is abstract and impossible to relate to on a personal level.

The ultimate idea of God in Buddhism is that of a void or emptiness. The following is written in one of the Sanskrit scriptures for Buddhism: "Why is there no obtaining of Nirvana? Because Nirvana is the realm of no 'thingness'. . . . If he is to realize Nirvana, he must pass beyond consciousness."[9] To say that Nirvana (the Buddhist equivalent of "heaven") is the realm of no thingness, or to say that we must pass beyond consciousness to realize Nirvana, is to make God out to be very abstract indeed.

By way of another example, the Quran says of Allah that "nothing is like Him" (*Surah* 42:11). Now, while a Christian would concur with such a statement (see Isaiah 40:18, 25; 55:8–9), Islam takes such a statement to an extreme. For example, one Muslim commentator writes, "So transcendent is the Divine Being [that He is] even above the limitation of metaphor."[10] If God is indeed unlike all metaphors and if there is no metaphor that communicates any truth about God in any sense, then it becomes impossible for humanity to conceive of what he is like. In essence, then, nothing can be known about God, which, again, is to push him away.[11]

Consequently, while many internationals will be very devoted to their religion, they can't honestly say they have a personal relationship with God. In fact, they may have difficulty even relating to such a concept. Nevertheless, they may very well be attracted to the personal relationship you have with God as a loving Father, wherein you pray to him, look to him for guidance, love him, and know that he loves you. The idea that we can cast all our anxiety on him because he cares for us (1 Peter 5:7) may be a new but powerful concept for them.

Moreover, keeping God's personhood in mind is often useful when addressing some objections. For example, it's helpful as a way by which to address the common belief that "there are as many paths to God as there are paths to the top of the mountain." How does God's personhood help here? Well, why is it true that there is only one way to God? Because our primary problem is not that of having to find our way to the top of a mountain; it is that we have broken our relationship with God because of our sin and rebellion against him.

So, in addressing the belief that there are many ways to God, pose the following question to your friend: "Assume that you are responsible for having broken a relationship with a friend because of a wrong, such as gossip or slander, you committed against him or her. How many ways are there to restore this relationship?" The answer is that there is really only one way to restore a broken relationship—by confessing our guilt and requesting our friend's forgiveness. This is the answer you come up with if you put their objection through the grid of God as one who has personal attributes.

APOLOGETICS AS DEFENSE

Defending the Source

The best place to attack anything is at its source, and in many respects the source of Christianity is the Bible. If the Bible can be shown to be false, then all of Christianity falls with it. Therefore, many internationals will attack the Bible, saying that it is nothing more than the mere words of men and that there is no merit to the claim that it is the unique Word of God.

Defending the authenticity of the Bible and its unique claim to being a revelation from God is a vast subject, and many approaches have been developed, but one that is especially useful is to point out the prescientific statements contained in the Bible.

Kenny Barfield, author of *Why the Bible Is Number One*, writes that "every ancient civilization and culture embraced scientific misconceptions in varying degrees, and biblical writers avoided those errors at a time when they were prevalent in secular documents."[12] And William Cairney, in a chapter titled "Biomedical Prescience 1" in *Evidence for Faith: Deciding the God Question*, writes, "By *prescience* we mean the occurrence, in Scripture, of accurate statements reflecting an in-depth knowledge of scientific concepts *far* before mankind had laid the technological base for such things to be known."[13]

The following examples, while not exhaustive, are some of the key prescientific statements found in the Bible. We take for granted many of the biblical views expressed below, but they were not the norm when they were written. In fact, the biblical views of the body, the nature of disease, the universe, and the earth went very much against the norm and were two thousand to three thousand years ahead of their time scientifically.

- The universe was thought to be enclosed, limited by some sort of solid barrier that surrounded the heavens. The biblical authors, however, depicted the universe not as being fixed or solid but as immense and capable of expansion (see Genesis 1:14; Job 26:7; Jeremiah 31:37; Zechariah 12:1).[14]
- In ancient times the universe was believed to be eternal and unchanging. And even in the twentieth century, scientists, including Einstein, did not want to concede to the increasing evidence that the universe was not eternal. But it is written in the Bible that "In the beginning God created the heavens and the earth" (Genesis 1:1).[15]

- Ancient authors wrote of the earth resting on various kinds of foundations, such as the backs of elephants, the top of a turtle or a catfish, or floating in a primal ocean, but Job wrote of the earth as being suspended over nothing (see Job 26:7).[16]
- The ocean floor was thought to be smooth, sandy, and lacking any usual geographical features, but the Bible speaks of "the valleys of the sea" (2 Samuel 22:16) and "the recesses of the deep" (Job 38:16). Barfield writes, "Not until the voyage of the *H.M.S. Challenger* in 1873 was the existence of underwater canyons documented by scientific research."[17]
- The authoritative voices in China, Babylon, Assyria, and Egypt asserted that only rain and rivers filled the ocean, but Moses, Job, and Solomon all wrote of springs or fountains in the deep that also contributed to the filling of the ocean (see Genesis 7:11; Job 38:16; Proverbs 8:28).[18]

The above evidence of prescientific statements calls for an explanation. Here we have several ancient documents in a collection, and these documents were written by different authors at different times and in different circumstances. All of the documents were written well before the modern scientific era. And yet included in these documents are accurate statements about scientific facts that were not discovered for another two thousand to three thousand years. Moreover, these biblical documents avoid errors that were commonly held in the surrounding cultures during the time of their writing. How can we explain this? It would seem that the best explanation is that the knowledge possessed by the biblical authors came from a source that was beyond them—perhaps a divine source, which is what their writings claim.

Addressing the Issue of Evolution

The teaching of evolution has crossed over into most, if not all, countries. You will find internationals from every country who believe in the theory of evolution. How should we address this issue?

Scientific theories concerning the origin of the universe and the diversity of life are looking more and more like the creation model than the naturalistic-evolutionary model.[19] Patrick Glynn, a former atheist turned theist, writes, "Ironically, the picture of the universe bequeathed to us by the most advanced twentieth-century science is closer in spirit to the vision presented in the Book of Genesis than anything offered by science since Copernicus."[20] We see this confirmed in several areas.

First, whereas scientists only seven decades ago believed that the universe was eternal, the theory of relativity, the second law of thermodynamics, and the red shift of the stars (which means they are moving away from us) indicate that the universe had a beginning. Moreover, the first law of thermodynamics, which speaks of the conservation of matter, implies that matter cannot just pop into existence but that something external to the universe must have caused it to come into existence. Since the universe cannot cause its own origin, its cause must lie outside itself.[21]

Second, when Charles Darwin's *The Origin of Species* was published in 1859, his theory predicted that there should be myriad transitional forms between the species in the fossil record. He considered the absence of such forms to be "the most obvious and gravest objection which can be urged against my theory."[22] But paleontology (the study of fossils) was a young science then, so Darwin was confident that the fossils of the transitional forms would eventually be found. They haven't. The gaps are still there. In fact, Stephen Jay Gould, a staunch supporter of the theory of evolution, had to come up with a revision of the theory to explain the gaps in the fossil record. He called it "punctuated equilibrium"—long periods where species remain substantially unchanged, interrupted by relatively short periods of rapid change.

Third, the idea that microevolution (minor changes) leads to macroevolution (major changes) through natural selection and mutation has not been demonstrated, even after decades of experimental breeding. For example, fruit flies are able to reproduce after only five days from birth, which means that a scientist can observe thousands of generations of fruit flies. While scientists have observed unusual variations being produced among the fruit flies, they have remained fruit flies nonetheless.[23] Even more, there is an upper limit to the changes that a species can sustain. When members of a species reach this limit, they become weaker, as creation of the "kinds" predicts—not stronger, as evolution predicts. While selective breeding and mutations can produce variations within a theme, the species stay "true to type,"[24] which is consistent with biblical teaching.

Fourth, following Stanley Miller's origin-of-life experiments in 1953, the scientific community was fairly confident that the chemical process whereby life arose from nonlife would soon be discovered. That process, however, has proven to be much more elusive than originally thought. For one thing, amino acids are among the basic building blocks for life. They are used to make the proteins that go into making the DNA that contains the information for life. Amino acids come in two forms—left-handed and right-handed. The problem is that living things use only left-handed amino acids. But experiments such as Miller's produce a random selection of both kinds of amino acids; they are unable to select only the left-handed kind, which means they are useless as a foundation for living things.[25] Those looking into the naturalistic processes supposedly responsible for the origin of life are no closer to a solution to such problems than they were fifty years ago. Michael Behe, a biochemist, wrote, "In private, many scientists admit that science has no explanation for the beginning of life."[26]

Fifth, there is an increasing body of evidence that reveals that random forces or the laws of nature simply are not sufficient as causes for such phenomena. What such evidence shows is the need to posit an intelligent designer as their explanation. For example, consider the extent to which the universe has been fine-tuned so as to bring about and sustain life.

- "Gravity is roughly 10^{39} times weaker than electromagnetism. If gravity had been 10^{33} times weaker than electromagnetism, 'stars would be a billion times less massive and would burn a million times faster.'"[27]
- "A stronger nuclear force (by as little as 2 percent) would have prevented the formation of protons—yielding a universe without atoms. Decreasing it by 5 percent would have given us a universe without stars."[28]
- "The very nature of water—so vital to life—is something of a mystery. . . . Unique among the molecules, water is lighter in

its solid than liquid form: Ice floats."[29] If it didn't, then the fish would die as they became trapped in the frozen water.

- Concerning the orbit of the earth, if it were slightly closer to the sun, all our water would boil away; if it were slightly farther away, all water would freeze. Bodily functions occur within a narrow temperature range, and earth is the right distance from the sun to fall within that range. Moreover, the orbit of the earth is more circular than elliptical, like other planets, which again causes the temperature to remain relatively even.[30]

Such examples go on and on. Is it indeed reasonable to think that such fine-tuning is the result of chance? As scientists played with various scenarios concerning the development of the universe, what they found was that "the most minuscule changes in the fundamental constants completely eliminated the possibility of life."[31] Rather than humanity appearing to be the result of blind, purposeless natural forces, such fine-tuning points more to the idea that we were intended to exist from the very beginning. As Patrick Glynn writes, "All the seemingly arbitrary and unrelated constants in physics have one thing in common—these are precisely the values you need if you want to have a universe capable of producing life."[32] Perhaps the constants are not so arbitrary and accidental after all; perhaps they were intentional. But intention is the characteristic of an intelligence, not of the blind and mindless forces of nature.

Besides the fine-tuning of the universe, another form of evidence for intelligent design is the irreducible complexity found on the molecular level. Michael Behe develops this approach in his book *Darwin's Black Box*. He quotes Darwin, "If it could be demonstrated that any complex organ existed which could not possibly have been formed by numerous, successive, slight modifications, my theory would absolutely break down."[33]

Is there such a system that would meet Darwin's criterion for falsifying his theory? Behe answers that a system that is "irreducibly complex" would meet such a criterion and that such systems can be found on the molecular level. Here's what Behe means by something being irreducibly complex: "a single system composed of several well-matched, interacting parts that contribute to the basic function, wherein the removal of any one of the parts causes the system to effectively cease functioning."[34]

There are basically two parts to this definition. First, an irreducibly complex system consists of multiple parts; and second, each part is essential to the functioning of the system. Behe illustrates this with the analogy of a mousetrap. A mousetrap consists of several parts, each of which is essential to its functioning. Moreover, each part needs to be in exact proportion to the other parts. For example, if the holding bar (the piece that holds the hammer down) is either too large or too small, the trap will not function.

One of the examples Behe develops is that of the chemical process by which blood clots. He summarizes it like this:

> The function of the blood-clotting system is as a strong, but transient barrier. The components of the system are ordered to that end. Fibronogen, plasminogen, thrombin, protein C, Christmas factor, and other components of the pathway together do something that none of the components can do alone. When vitamin K is unavailable or antihemophilic factor is missing, the system crashes just as surely as a Rube Goldberg machine fails if a component is missing.[35]

Why does Behe think that such irreducibly complex systems meet Darwin's own criteria for proving the theory of evolution wrong? Because such complex and interrelated systems are useless unless they are complete, and their completeness cannot happen as a result of small, gradual changes.[36] But the idea that such small, gradual changes did indeed take place lies at the foundation of evolutionary theory.

Finally, DNA exhibits a characteristic that goes far beyond what can be produced by the random processes of nature—and this characteristic is information, which is unique to intelligence. The DNA in a single cell contains as much information as a 90–120 volume encyclopedia.[37] Can such information indeed rise from natural forces alone, or is an intelligent agent required?

Consider the fact that natural phenomena can be explained through one of only three possibilities—random forces, laws of nature, or intelligent design. Phenomena produced by random forces are characterized by irregular patterns and contain no information. Phenomena produced by the laws of nature are characterized as being regular, repeatable, and predictable (for example, patterns formed in the sand by the movement of ocean waves), but they contain little, if any, information. Phenomena produced by intelligent design are characterized as being unpredictable and irregular but as containing specified information (for example, the words "Dean loves Debbie" written on the beach).[38]

The evidence of the fine-tuning of the universe, the irreducible complexity on the molecular level, and the information contained in DNA point to the fact that the naturalistic-evolutionary model is insufficient as an explanation for the wonder of life and point instead to the need to include an intelligent designer in our hypothesis.

APOLOGETICS AS OFFENSE

For apologetics to be effective, it should not be only attractive and defensive but offensive as well. By *offensive* I do not mean that we intend to offend others, but that we intend to sensitively and gently point out the weaknesses in their argument or worldview. The following are some ways by which to do this.

Turn Their Arguments In on Themselves

Many internationals have been just as influenced by relativistic perspectives as those in the West. The way to respond to such relativistic statements is by turning them in on themselves and seeing what happens. The following are some examples:

- "While it's fine for you to believe that Christianity is true for you, that doesn't mean it's true for me." Persons who make such a statement are coming from a relativistic perspective that says there is no absolute truth that applies to all people universally. But such a relativistic statement claims to be an absolute truth, thereby refuting itself. Also, persons who make such a statement claim to be an exception to their own rule, for they are making an absolute claim that there is no absolute truth.[39]

- "The scientific method is the only reliable path to truth. Unless something can be proven scientifically, I will not believe it." Such a statement is itself a philosophical one and thereby goes beyond the bounds of its own criterion for truth, which is scientific observation.
- "It is wrong to judge others." Persons making such a statement are judging you for judging others. Again, such persons are claiming to be an exception to their own rule. They are saying that it is wrong for a Christian to declare another worldview to be wrong.[40]
- "Christians are intolerant." If what these persons mean by *intolerant* is to not accept all claims to truth as being equally true, then they are not living up to their own standard, for they do not accept the Christian teachings as being true.[41]
- "The country in which you were born pretty much determines what religion you will follow." Such a statement says nothing about which religion is true. Moreover, the argument could be used against persons who make the statement, because they have been influenced by their culture as well.[42]

Another way of responding to such relativistic beliefs is to ask the international to imagine applying these same relativistic beliefs to some field of science, such as aerospace engineering. What would the professor think if you were to write on your final exam the following statements?

- I believe that all aerospace theories are basically the same.
- I believe that a theory might be true for you—the professor—but not for me.
- I believe that we should not make judgments about the truthfulness of various theories.

The student would probably be kicked out of the program, and for good reason. After all, no one would want to fly on a plane designed by such a relativistic scientist. But if it is obviously absurd to apply such relativistic statements to the physical sciences, then why is it not also absurd when someone applies them to all of reality?[43]

Expose the Practice of Borrowing from a Worldview While at the Same Time Arguing against It

Some internationals will argue that reincarnation is more just than is the Christian teaching that we will be judged after one lifetime. But the question must be asked, On what do they base their concept of justice? Reincarnation is based on the *impersonal principle* of the law of cause and effect (or karma), which means that we each reap what we sow and that there are no exceptions to the rule. The laws of karma are similar to the laws of nature in that both are based on impersonal forces. Moreover, reincarnation is most often—and most consistently—taught in the context of ultimate reality being impersonal. Otherwise there would be a place for the forgiveness of our actions, and this isn't usually something found in the teaching of reincarnation.

But justice, unlike karma, is an attribute of personal beings. Justice is similar to reincarnation in that both connect consequences to actions, but they are different in that justice is based on a moral foundation that declares some actions to be right and others to be wrong. Reincarnation, on the other hand, only connects actions to consequences, but since it is in the context of ultimate reality being a oneness beyond all distinctions (including moral distinctions), it does not have a sufficient foundation to determine which actions are right and which are wrong. They are merely actions that carry consequences, and nothing more. Only a theistic worldview, such as Christianity, has a sufficient moral foundation to sustain the concept of justice. Therefore, those who say that reincarnation is more just than the Christian teaching on God's judgment are in fact borrowing from the Christian worldview while at the same time arguing against it, thereby giving tacit confirmation to the very thing they are arguing against.

Another objection internationals sometimes lodge against Christianity is that of the problem of evil, which questions the existence of God because of the presence of so much evil and suffering in the world. How can a good God allow such evil and suffering? But, again, they are borrowing from the very belief system they are claiming to argue against. As Paul Copan writes, "The presence of evil presupposes the existence of an objective moral standard that is being violated. If real evil exists, then an objective standard of goodness by which something is deemed evil must also exist"[44]—and this objective standard of goodness is found only in a holy God, which is precisely what they are arguing against.

Be Aware of Moving from One System of Thought to an Opposing System of Thought

This principle is similar to the previous one in which an international borrows an element from the Christian worldview while arguing against it. But it's slightly different in that the international makes a seamless transition from one system of thought to an opposing system of thought without even being aware that he or she has made the move. While one technique borrows from a worldview, the other makes a move into the worldview.

For example, one Muslim international student objected to the gospel by saying that it didn't seem fair that *Jesus* would have to pay for *our* sins. Such a belief, he contended, goes totally against God's justice. In response, I asked, "We both agree that God is just and holy. So what then will happen to you on Judgment Day when you face this just and holy God?" The student responded, "I hope God will forgive me. I repent every day of my sins and ask for God's forgiveness."

Did you catch it? This student moved from talking about God being just to God being forgiving, while at the same time denying the biblical foundation for God's forgiveness, which is Christ's substitutionary death on the cross.

I asked the student, "But why should God forgive you? After all, you said yourself that God is just and holy. So if we've broken God's law, how would it be just for God to forgive us? What we deserve is judgment, not forgiveness. Also, you need to realize that forgiveness comes at a price, and it's a price that is beyond our ability to pay. The religion of Islam does not provide for anyone to pay the price of forgiveness. If God forgives without paying the price for forgiveness, then his holiness is diminished. But in Christianity, Christ is the one who paid the price on our behalf."

To give another example, one international objected to Christianity by saying, "It's unfair that Christians are forgiven when others whose lives may have been very exemplary receive judgment." Did you catch the move? Notice carefully what is being said here. This person is in effect saying that "those who live exemplary lives deserve to be forgiven at least as much as, if not more than, Christians deserve to be forgiven." What this international is doing is moving from the language of grace ("forgiveness") to the language of merit ("exemplary lives"). By pointing to the exemplary lives of those in other religions as qualifying them for forgiveness, this person is coming from the mistaken notion that forgiveness is something to be earned. But do Christians deserve to be forgiven? No. Does anyone deserve to be forgiven? No. Why not? Because forgiveness is not something to be earned or deserved. "Deserved forgiveness" is a contradiction in terms. It is the mixing of two opposing languages—the language of grace and the language of merit—for a gift can only be received, never earned.

SOME FINAL ADVICE

Be patient. As you can imagine, changing the religion or worldview that one has grown up with is not easy, and it often takes time. At least initially as you are developing your apologetic/evangelist skills, focus on a single segment of the international population who come from one religion or worldview. In other words, if possible, focus on Buddhists, or Hindus, or Muslims, or secularists. Why? Because it will be enough of a challenge to become adept at dealing with the issues presented by any one religion or worldview. Plus, as you develop skills in working with one group, these skills will be transferable to working with other groups later on.

Read widely in the religion or worldview on which you are focusing. Read both the literature promoting this religion or worldview and the literature opposing it. If you find your faith being threatened by such reading, either stop reading it or find a mature Christian who can guide you through it.

Pray fervently. While we as humans can address the intellectual and emotional issues, the deeper battle has to do with the person's heart and will, and only the Holy Spirit can touch those areas of a person's life.

Affirm with your international friend that your friendship is unconditional and that it will never be contingent on what he or she does with Jesus Christ.

Introduce your international friend to other Christians. The international is more likely to come to the Lord when he or she sees the effect the Lord has had on the lives of several Christians rather than on just one.

QUESTIONS FOR REFLECTION AND DISCUSSION

1. If we aren't consciously looking for the internationals among us, we often fail to notice them. Talk about the pockets of internationals who live among you. Where are they? They may be at your work, in your neighborhood, or in the schools around you. What nationalities are they? What religions are they? Also, mention the internationals you know personally.

2. Friendship is the first step in evangelizing an international. What are some ways you can build the bridge of friendship with the internationals around you?

3. Discuss the points of attraction mentioned in the "Apologetics as Attraction" section. Can you think of other points of attraction to the gospel? What other movies or books would be a good means by which to get the discussion started and to illustrate the gospel?

4. Besides the two objections addressed in the "Apologetics as Defense" section (attacks against the Bible and against the Creator), what other objections have you encountered? What suggestions do you have for addressing them?

5. If someone persists in believing in the theory of evolution, do you think that such a belief prevents them from accepting the gospel?

6. What objections have you encountered that commit fallacious forms of reasoning similar to the ones found in the "Apologetics as Offense" section?

Appendix:
Church Leaders' Annotated
Resource Guide

CHAPTER 1: THE PASTOR
AS AN APOLOGIST

Chang, Curtis. *Engaging Unbelief: A Captivating Strategy from Augustine and Aquinas*. Downers Grove, Ill.: InterVarsity Press, 2000. Augustine's and Aquinas's unique responses to the threats to Christianity in their days not only strengthened the church but, even more, won over their critics. The author illustrates how their wise and winsome apologetic can speak to our postmodern world.

Hafemann, Scott. *The God of Promise and the Life of Faith: Understanding the Heart of the Bible*. Wheaton, Ill.: Crossway, 2001. A pastor and professor, Scott Hafemann offers a comprehensive view of the grand scope of the Bible through the lens of faith, hope, and love. He writes with pastoral sensitivity, especially regarding suffering and longing.

Stewart, James. *A Faith to Proclaim*. Grand Rapids: Baker, 1953.

———. *Heralds of God*. Grand Rapids: Baker, 1972. Along with *A Faith to Proclaim*, a treasure of exposition and illustrations combining biblical studies and literary allusions. James Stewart was truly one of the great preachers and writers of his time. Although his books are out of print, see http://www.abe.com for these and other out-of-print works.

Turnbull, Ralph G. *A Minister's Obstacles*. Grand Rapids: Baker, 1972.

———. *A Minister's Opportunities*. Grand Rapids: Baker, 1979. Another classic set of books by "a pastor to pastors," dealing with the personal and professional life of the minister. Turnbull probes the challenges and privileges before the pastor under such headings as "The Beauty of Holiness" and "The Sense of What Is Vital." Out of print but available through http://www.abe.com

Zacharias, Ravi. *Jesus Among Other Gods: The Absolute Claims of the Christian Message*. Nashville: Word, 2000. The author examines Jesus' distinctive response to six questions that no one else claiming divine or prophetic status would have answered in such a manner. He particularly looks at the uniqueness of Jesus' character and his apologetic approach.

_____. *Three Severe Tests for Ministry* (audiotape). This sermon looks at Paul's defense of his ministry in Corinth under severe conditions. Three critical tests for an authentic ministry and life are examined. See http://www.rzim.org

CHAPTER 2: FOUR CHALLENGES FOR CHURCH LEADERS

Carnell, Edward J. *An Introduction to Christian Apologetics: A Philosophic Defense of the Trinitarian-Theistic Faith*. Grand Rapids: Eerdmans, 1948. Out of print but an essential, classic work by one of the most influential apologists of the twentieth century. See http://www.abe.com

Carson, D. A., ed. *Telling the Truth: Evangelizing Postmoderns*. Grand Rapids: Zondervan, 2000. A compilation of messages delivered at a conference on evangelizing postmoderns held at Trinity Evangelical Divinity School. A practical, balanced resource offering tools and insights for ministering in our postmodern climate.

Chesterton, G. K. *Orthodoxy*. San Francisco: Ignatius Press, 1995. One of the most significant defenses of the Christian faith ever written. His writings have had a profound influence on many thinking Christians, including C. S. Lewis.

Geisler, Norman. *Baker Encyclopedia of Apologetics*, Baker Reference Library. Grand Rapids: Baker, 1999. An exhaustive one-volume edition on apologetics representing a lifetime of study and ministry by Norman Geisler. The encyclopedia includes entries for key issues, philosophers, and difficult Bible passages.

Geisler, Norman, and Ronald Brooks. *Come, Let Us Reason: An Introduction to Logical Thinking.* Grand Rapids: Baker, 1990. The authors provide a readable primer on logic and the assumptions we make based on reasoning (or faulty reasoning).

Guinness, Os. *God in the Dark: The Assurance of Faith Beyond a Shadow of a Doubt.* Wheaton, Ill.: Crossway, 1996. Guinness observes, "Doubt is not primarily an abstract philosophical or theological question.... At its most basic, doubt is a matter of truth, trust and trustworthiness. Can we trust God? Are we sure?" Written to the believer wrestling with doubt.

_____. *Long Journey Home: A Guide to Your Search for the Meaning of Life.* Colorado Springs/New York: Waterbrook Press/Doubleday, 2001. Traversing similar territory as *God in the Dark* but written to the seeker who is moving toward belief. A poignant look at the interior lives of well-known people—some who rejected Christianity and others who embraced it.

McGrath, Alister. *Intellectuals Don't Need God and Other Modern Myths.* Grand Rapids: Zondervan, 1993. Written to those who are not convinced by the arguments of classical apologetics and who believe that for Christianity to be persuasive to non-Christians, it must have a broader appeal than to reason alone.

Zacharias, Ravi. *Can Man Live Without God?* Dallas: Word, 1994. A compendium of lectures delivered at Harvard University and Ohio State University. The book is a response to the questions "Does God exist?" "Who is Jesus?" and "What gives life meaning?"

_____. *Christian Apologetics and the Modern Mind.* In this audiotape series Zacharias introduces the task, nature, and necessity of apologetics. The two lectures were delivered to the Irish Congress on Evangelism. Available at http://www.rzim.org

CHAPTER 3: THE CHURCH AS THE HEART AND SOUL OF APOLOGETICS

(A fuller description of these books and their authors appears in this chapter.)
Behe, Michael. *Darwin's Black Box: The Biochemical Challenge to Evolution.* New York: Touchstone, 1998.

Johnson, Phillip. *Darwin on Trial.* Downers Grove, Ill.: InterVarsity Press, 1993. In these two books professors Michael Behe and Phillip Johnson examine the often unchallenged assumptions of Darwinian theory and provide extraordinary intellectual ammunition for apologetics in the fields of evolution and creation.

Lewis, C. S. *Mere Christianity.* New York: HarperCollins, 2001, reprint; first published, 1952. A classic statement blending philosophical reason and moral imperatives with the claims of Christ.

McDowell, Josh. *More Than a Carpenter.* Wheaton, Ill.: Tyndale House, 1987. McDowell analyzes Christ's claims under C. S. Lewis's headings of whether he was liar, lunatic, or Lord.

Strobel, Lee. *The Case for Christ: A Journalist's Personal Investigation of the Evidence for Jesus.* Grand Rapids: Zondervan, 1998. This former *Chicago Tribune* reporter won a Gold Medallion Book Award for this probing book. Strobel has two chapters on the "Tough Questions about Christ" in *Who Made God?* (the companion volume to *Is Your Church Ready?*).

CHAPTER 4: THE PRIORITY OF APOLOGETICS IN THE CHURCH

Crabb, Larry. *Finding God.* Grand Rapids: Zondervan, 1993. An intensely personal book written on the heels of his own brother's death, Christian psychologist Larry Crabb examines the obstacles that keep us from finding God.

Craig, William Lane. *No Easy Answers: Finding Hope in Doubt, Failure, and Unanswered Prayer.* Chicago: Moody Press, 1990. A Christian philosopher (who has a chapter in the companion volume *Who Made God?*) offers compelling wisdom for the believer struggling with difficult questions.

The Faith and Science Lecture Forum. For information, visit http://www.faithandscience.com/home.html

Grant, Peter. Teaching tapes from Cumberland Community Church. "Tough Questions Answered" (Ref # S0018–0022) is a 4-part audiotape series dealing with tough questions about faith, doubt, and suffering. "God, I Have a Question!" (Ref # S9809–9815) is a

7-part audiotape series dealing with evidences for the existence of God, reliability of the Bible, deity of Christ, and so on. These are available from Cumberland Community Church, 3110 Sports Ave., Smyrna, GA 30080; phone 770-952-8834; on the Web at http:// www.cumberlandchurch.org

Habermas, Gary. *Dealing with Doubt.* Chicago: Moody Press, 1990. Habermas shows that doubt is not only a "lack of certainty concerning the teachings of Christianity" but also a lack of understanding the existential significance of these teachings in one's life.

Hunter III, George G. *How to Reach Secular People.* Nashville: Abingdon, 1992. This book looks at four models for how secular people become Christians.

Lewis, C. S. *The Problem of Pain.* New York: HarperCollins, 2001, reprint; first published, 1940. This book contains Lewis's memorable insight: "God whispers to us in our pleasures . . . but shouts in our pains: it is His megaphone to rouse a deaf world."

Petersen, Jim. *Living Proof: Sharing the Gospel Naturally.* Colorado Springs: NavPress, 1989. Petersen draws on his many years of work with The Navigators to assist readers in developing relationships with the unreached.

Watson, David. *My God Is Real.* Eastbourne, England: Kingsway, 1985. A popular British author writes to both believer and unbeliever. An engaging and classic defense of the reality of God and his transforming power in our lives.

CHAPTER 5: ARROWS AND SWORDS IN THE CHURCH

Akers, John, John Armstrong, and John Woodbridge, eds. *This We Believe: The Good News of Jesus Christ for the World.* Grand Rapids: Zondervan, 2000. What is the Good News, and how do we mirror its message? This book is a pastoral commentary on the key themes of the declaration "The Gospel of Jesus Christ: An Evangelical Celebration," found in its entirety in the appendix of the book.

Green, Michael. *Evangelism in the Early Church.* Grand Rapids: Eerdmans, 1980. Green examines the obstacles to the gospel that the early church faced and the various means it employed to overcome them and preach the gospel. Includes a wealth of primary sources and rich biographical illustrations from the early church. Out of print but available through http://www.abe.com

Zacharias, Ravi. *Flirting with the Truth* (audiotape). Four worldviews collide in Paul's time, yet the apostle, standing before Felix, uses gentleness and persuasion to bring Felix to common ground and a point of reference.

_____. *The Lostness of Man* (audiotape). Delivered at Amsterdam '86 (the Billy Graham Evangelistic Association's conference on evangelism), this sermon explores the reality that "the fundamental problem of man is his very heart." See http://www.rzim.org

CHAPTER 6: CREATING AN APOLOGETIC CLIMATE IN THE HOME

Diaz, Gwendolyn. *Sticking Up for What I Believe: Answers to the Spiritual Questions Teenagers Ask.* Colorado Springs: NavPress, 2002. Based on conversations the author—an Ivy-League graduate—had with her sons, *Sticking Up for What I Believe* encourages teens to understand and defend their faith, helping them answer such questions as "Can you prove there's a God?" and "Is the Bible true?"

James, Carolyn Custis. *When Life and Beliefs Collide.* Grand Rapids: Zondervan, 2001. James weaves the stories of everyday women with the lives of Mary and Martha in this deeply compelling book. She reveals the practicality of knowing God truly and inspires men and women to sit at the feet of Jesus, that we may be equipped and empowered to face the realities of life and offer strength, hope, and wisdom to our families, friends, and churches.

Morley, Donna. *A Christian Woman's Guide to Understanding Mormonism.* Eugene, Ore.: Harvest House, 2003.

Salisbury, Judy. *A Christian Woman's Guide to Reasons for Faith.* Eugene, Ore.: Harvest House, 2003.

Wallace, Ronald. *Hannah's Prayer and Its Answer: An Exposition for Bible Study and Church.* Grand Rapids: Eerdmans, 2002. Renowned Bible teacher Ronald Wallace explores this memorable mother's prayer and demonstrates its contemporary relevance for all. A scholarly yet readable work intended for church or personal study.

Apologetic Resources for Children and Teens

Geisler, Norman, and Ron Brooks. *When Skeptics Ask: A Handbook on Christian Evidences.* Grand Rapids: Baker, 1995, reissue). For middle school students and older.

Geisler, Norman, and Joseph Holden. *Living Loud: Defending Your Faith.* Nashville: Broadman & Holman, 2002.

McDowell, Josh. *Don't Check Your Brains at the Door.* Dallas: Word, 1992.

_____. *More Than a Carpenter* (Wheaton, Ill.: Tyndale House, 1987). McDowell analyzes Christ's claims under C. S. Lewis's headings of whether he was liar, lunatic, or Lord. McDowell's books, as well as other apologetics resources, are available at http://www.josh.org

_____. *The Resurrection Factor* (audiotapes). Without the resurrection, our faith is futile. This 3-tape set offers a thorough study of the evidence supporting the resurrection of Jesus Christ.

_____. *Right from Wrong.* Dallas: Word, 1994. Absolute truth based on the attributes of God; available for elementary children as well as youth.

Waller, Lynn. *How Do We Know the Bible Is True? Reasons a Kid Can Believe It.* Grand Rapids: Zondervan, 1991. Little-known, fun facts about the Bible show eight- to twelve-year-olds why the Bible is trustworthy.

CHAPTER 7: OFF TO COLLEGE: CAN WE KEEP THEM?

Boundless Webzine, the online magazine for Christian college students, published by Focus on the Family at http://www.boundless.org

Budziszewski, J. *How to Stay Christian in College: An Interactive Guide.* Colorado Springs: NavPress, 1999. Writing out of his own experience of abandoning his faith upon entering college, Budziszewski sympathizes with the unique obstacles Christian students face.

Christian Classics Ethereal Library, an exhaustive electronic library of works by Christians throughout the ages, is located at Calvin College (http://www.ccel.org). The CCEL was previously located at Wheaton College (1995–99) and at the University of Pittsburgh (1993–95).

Leadership U, the resource website for Christian college students maintained by Christian Leadership Ministries, an affiliate of Campus Crusade for Christ at http://www.leaderu.com

Morris, Thomas V. *Philosophy for Dummies.* Hoboken, N.J.: Wiley, 1999. An easily accessible—and often witty—primer outlining the basics of philosophy by a Christian philosopher.

Sire, James W. *Chris Chrisman Goes to College: And Faces the Challenges of Relativism, Individualism and Pluralism.* Downers Grove, Ill.: InterVarsity Press, 1993. A lively depiction of a fictional character's first year at college with corresponding chapters unpacking the various challenges he encounters.

CHAPTER 8: ISSUES AND APPROACHES IN WORKING WITH INTERNATIONALS

(Annotations are not provided due to number of resources listed.)

Apologetics

Copan, Paul. *"True for You, but Not for Me": Deflating the Slogans That Leave Christians Speechless.* Minneapolis: Bethany House, 1998.

Corduan, Winfried. *No Doubt About It: The Case for Christianity.* Nashville: Broadman & Holman, 1997.

Geisler, Norman, and Ron Brooks. *When Skeptics Ask: A Handbook on Christian Evidences.* Grand Rapids: Baker, 1995, reissue.

Geisler, Norman, and Paul Hoffman, eds. *Why I Am a Christian: Leading Thinkers Explain Why They Believe,* Grand Rapids: Baker, 2001.

Kreeft, Peter. *Yes or No: Straight Answers to Tough Questions About Christianity.* San Francisco: Ignatius Press, 1991.

Kreeft, Peter, and Ronald Tacelli. *Handbook of Christian Apologetics.* Downers Grove, Ill.: InterVarsity Press, 1994.

Strobel, Lee. *The Case for Faith.* Grand Rapids: Zondervan, 2000.

Buddhism

Sonrise Center for Buddhist Studies, http://www.sonrisecenter.org/services.html

Zacharias, Ravi. *The Lotus and the Cross: Jesus Talks with Buddha.* Sisters, Ore.: Multnomah, 2001.

Evangelism

Pollard, Nick. *Evangelism Made Slightly Less Difficult: How to Interest People Who Aren't Interested.* Downers Grove, Ill.: InterVarsity Press, 1997.

Richardson, Rick. *Evangelism Outside the Box: New Ways to Help People Experience the Good News.* Downers Grove, Ill.: InterVarsity Press, 2000.

Schneider, Floyd. *Evangelism for the Fainthearted.* Grand Rapids: Kregel, 2000.

Evolution, Arguments against

Access Research Network, http://arn.org

Broom, Neil. *How Blind Is the Watchmaker? Nature's Design and the Limits of Naturalistic Science.* Downers Grove, Ill.: InterVarsity Press, 2001.

Denton, Michael. *Evolution: A Theory in Crisis.* Bethesda, Md.: Adler & Adler, 1985.

Discovery Institute: Center for the Renewal of Science and Culture, www.discovery.org/crsc

Wells, Jonathan. *Icons of Evolution: Science or Myth?* Washington, D.C.: Regnery, 2000.

Hinduism

Brooke, Tal. *Riders of the Cosmic Circuit.* Batavia, Ill.: Lion, 1986.

Karma to Grace (Winfried Corduan), http://www.karma2grace.org

Maharaj, Rabindranath. *Death of a Guru: A Hindu Comes to Christ.* Eugene, Ore.: Harvest House, 1986.

International Student Ministry

Association of Christians Ministering among Internationals (ACMI), http://www.gateman.com/acmi/index2.html

International Students, Inc., http://www.isionline.org

InterVarsity's International Student Ministry, http://www.ivcf.org/ism

Phillips, Tom, and Bob Norsworthy. *The World at Your Door: Reaching International Students in Your Home, Church, and School.* Minneapolis: Bethany House, 1997.

Islam

Answering Islam, http://answering-islam.org

Geisler, Norman, and Abdul Saleeb. *Answering Islam: The Crescent in the Light of the Cross.* Grand Rapids: Baker, 1993.

Gilchrist, John. *Facing the Muslim Challenge: A Handbook of Christian-Muslim Dialogue.* Benoni, South Africa: Muslim Evangelism Resource Centre of Southern Africa, 1999.

McCurry, Don. *Healing the Broken Family of Abraham: New Life for Muslims.* Colorado Springs: Ministries to Muslims, 2001.

Middle East Resources, http://www.safeplace.net/members/mer

Saal, William. *Reaching Muslims for Christ.* Chicago: Moody Press, 1991.

Shahid, Samuel. *The Cross or the Crescent,* video and training manual. North American Mission Board of the Southern Baptist Convention, 2001 (http://www.namb.net). Call 866-407-6262 for this and other resources.

World Religions

Halverson, Dean, ed. *The Compact Guide to World Religions.* Minneapolis: Bethany House, 1996.

Netland, Harold. *Dissonant Voices: Religious Pluralism and the Question of Truth.* Grand Rapids: Eerdmans, 1991.

———. *Encountering Religious Pluralism: The Challenge to Christian Faith and Mission.* Downers Grove, Ill.: InterVarsity Press, 2001.

Ridenour, Fritz. *So What's the Difference? A Look at 20 Worldviews, Faiths and Religions and How They Compare to Christianity.* Ventura, Calif.: Regal, 2001.

NOTES

Chapter 2.
Four Challenges for Church Leaders

[1] An important fine-tuning of this has been done by Norman L. Geisler in his book *Christian Apologetics* (Grand Rapids: Baker, 1988). See his chapter 8, "Formulating Adequate Tests for Truth."

[2] Peter Kreeft, *Three Philosophies of Life* (San Francisco: Ignatius Press, 1989), 54.

Chapter 3.
The Church as the Heart and Soul of Apologetics

[1] Cited in Kenneth L. Woodward, "Gospel on the Potomac," *Newsweek* (10 March 2003), 29.

[2] Dorothy Sayers, *Creed or Chaos?* (New York: Harcourt Brace, 1949).

[3] Allan Bloom, *The Closing of the American Mind: How Higher Education Has Failed Democracy and Impoverished the Souls of Today's Students* (New York: Simon & Schuster, 1987).

[4] C. S. Lewis, *Mere Christianity* (New York: HarperCollins, 2001, reprint; first published, 1952), 52.

[5] Lee Strobel, *The Case for Christ* (Grand Rapids: Zondervan, 1998).

[6] Phillip E. Johnson, *Darwin on Trial,* 2d ed. (Downers Grove, Ill.: InterVarsity Press, 1993); Michael J. Behe, *Darwin's Black Box* (New York: Free Press, 1996).

[7] C. S. Lewis, *Mere Christianity* (New York: HarperCollins, 2001, reprint; first published, 1952).

8 Josh McDowell, *More Than a Carpenter* (Wheaton, Ill.: Tyndale House, 1987).

Chapter 4.
The Priority of Apologetics in the Church

1 See, for example, Acts 1:3; 5:40; 6:9, 11; 15:7; 16:15; 17:2, 4, 17; 18:4, 13–14, 19; 19:8–9, 26; 23:9; 24:12; 25:14, 16; 26:9, 25–26, 28; 28:20, 23–24.

2 Several years ago we started just such a ministry at Cumberland Community Church called "Reasons for Faith." This ministry hosts classes and seminars at the popular level and seminary level, in addition to sponsoring debates. Information can be obtained by writing Cumberland Community Church, 3110 Sports Dr., Smyrna, GA 30080-3958.

3 Ravi Zacharias and Norman Geisler, eds., *Who Made God? And Answers to Over 100 Other Tough Questions of Faith* (Grand Rapids: Zondervan, 2003).

4 Jim Petersen, *Living Proof: Sharing the Gospel Naturally* (Colorado Springs: NavPress, 1989), 188–89.

5 See Figure 4.1. George Hunter, dean at the E. Stanley Jones School of Evangelism and World Mission, Asbury Theological Seminary, lists ten characteristics of secular people that explain the kind of difficult questions they often have: (1) Secular people are essentially ignorant of basic Christianity. (2) Secular people are seeking life before death. (3) Secular people are conscious of doubt more than guilt. (4) Secular people have a negative image of the church. (5) Secular people have multiple alienations. (6) Secular people are untrusting. (7) Secular people have low self-esteem. (8) Secular people experience forces in history as "out of control." (9) Secular people experience forces in personality as "out of control." (10) Secular people cannot find "the door" to the church (George G. Hunter III, *How to Reach Secular People* [Nashville: Abingdon, 1992], 44–54). This "cultural chasm" can also be applied to the outsiders' experience when they start attending church—"boring" church services, unfamiliar

language, outdated music, and antiquated (and often shabby) surroundings. They experience a different culture from the one they are used to—and issues such as caring, "cringing," credibility, creativity, and comfort become barriers. For further discussion, see this author's doctoral thesis, *The Tension Between Biblical Purity and Cultural Relevance in Seeker Churches,* which is available through Cumberland Community Church.

6 A form of this diagram first came to the author's attention through the ministry of Reaching the Unchurched Network in the United Kingdom (http://www.run.org.uk).

7 C. S. Lewis, *Mere Christianity* (New York: HarperCollins, 2001, reprint; first published, 1952), 39.

8 This treatment of doubt is directed at the seeker; for a treatment relevant to the believer see chapter 1 in William Lane Craig's *No Easy Answers: Finding Hope in Doubt, Failure and Unanswered Prayer* (Chicago: Moody Press, 1990), 29–41.

9 Gary Habermas, *Dealing with Doubt* (Chicago: Moody Press, 1990), 10.

10 Os Guinness, *Doubt: Faith in Two Minds,* 2d ed. (Glasgow, Scotland: Collins, 1983), 27. (Reprinted as *God in the Dark* [Wheaton, Ill.: Crossway, 1996]).

11 David Watson, *My God Is Real* (Eastbourne, Eng.: Kingsway, 1985), 78.

12 John 5:24 says, "I tell you the truth, whoever hears my word and believes him who sent me has eternal life and will not be condemned; he has crossed over from death to life."

13 See James 1:2–18, on how trials build our faith to bring about perseverance, maturity, and completeness. Indeed, James implies that, if anyone can't see this, he must ask God for wisdom to see how trials build us up: "But when he asks, *he must believe and not doubt,* because he who doubts is like a wave of the sea, blown and tossed by the wind" (James 1:6, italics added). Matthew 14:31 tells us of Jesus' rebuke of Peter for Peter's lack of faith during a storm: "Immediately Jesus reached out his hand and caught him. 'You of little faith,' he said, 'why did you doubt?'" In another example, Abraham is tested with regard to his son

Isaac. God says in Genesis 22:12, "Now I know that you fear
God, because you have not withheld from me your son, your
only son."

[14] Larry Crabb, *Finding God* (Grand Rapids: Zondervan, 1993), 71.

[15] An application of the truth of 2 Corinthians 1:3–7.

[16] C. S. Lewis, *The Problem of Pain* (New York: HarperCollins, 2001,
reprint; first published, 1940), 91.

Chapter 5.
Arrows and Swords in the Church

[1] Cited in Michael Green, *Evangelism in the Early Church* (Grand
Rapids: Eerdmans, 1983), 203.

[2] C. S. Lewis, *The Screwtape Letters* (New York: HarperCollins, 2001,
reprint; originally published, 1942), 135.

[3] Arthur Peacocke, "New Wineskins for Old Wine: A Credible
Theology for a Scientific World," in *Science & Spirit,* vol. 10
(1999), 32.

[4] William Barclay, *The Letters to the Corinthians,* Daily Bible Study
Series, revised edition (Philadelphia: Westminster, 1975), 2.

[5] William Temple, *Readings in St. John's Gospel* (London: Macmillan,
1940), 68.

Chapter 6.
Creating an Apologetic Climate in the Home

[1] These resources, as well as those specifically written to mothers,
are listed in the appendix at the back of the book. To help meet
the challenge of making apologetics accessible, I wrote *A Christian Woman's Guide to Reasons for Faith.*

[2] See, for example, Apologetic Resources for Children and Teens in
the appendix.

[3] Dottie and Josh McDowell, with David Nathan Weiss, *The Topsy-
Turvy Kingdom* (Wheaton, Ill.: Tyndale for Kids, 1996).

⁴ *The Resurrection Debate with Dr. Dale Miller,* available at Walter
  Martin's Religious InfoNet, http://www.waltermartin.com,
  or write Box 25710, St. Paul, MN 55125.
⁵ Lee Strobel, *The Case for Christ* (Grand Rapids: Zondervan, 1998).
⁶ For more information on Community Bible Study, visit
  http://www.communitybiblestudy.org, or call 1-800-826-4181.
  For Bible Study Fellowship, visit
  http://www.bsfinternational.org, or call 877-273-3228. For
  Precept Ministries, visit http://www.precept.org, or call
  1-800-763-8280.
⁷ If you are hard-pressed to find a female apologist who can speak
  to the women of your fellowship, I would enjoy the opportunity.
  To reach me, contact Logos Presentations, 11500 NE 76th St.
  A3–202, Vancouver, WA 98662 (e-mail at logos@wa-net.com).
⁸ J. P. Moreland, *Love Your God with All Your Mind* (Colorado
  Springs: NavPress, 1997), 131.

Chapter 7.
Off to College: Can We Keep Them?

¹ My academic subject is ethical and political philosophy, focusing
  on natural law and on religion in public life.
² The column "Office Hours" appears in *Boundless Webzine*
  (http://www.boundless.org).
³ See the appendix for the resource list for this chapter.
⁴ John R. W. Stott, *You Can Trust the Bible* (Grand Rapids: Discovery
  House, 1982), 14.
⁵ The following three paragraphs are adapted from my article
  "What's Good about Sex?" in *Citizen* magazine (November
  1999).
⁶ Some helpful reflections about this combination are offered in
  Ben Young and Sam Adams, *The Ten Commandments of Dating*
  (Nashville: Nelson, 1999).
⁷ "For you have died, and your life is hid with Christ in God.
  When Christ who is our life appears, then you also will appear
  with him in glory" (Colossians 3:3–4 RSV). "Beloved, we are

God's children now; it does not yet appear what we shall be, but we know that when he appears we shall be like him, for we shall see him as he is" (1 John 3:2 RSV). "To him who conquers I will give some of the hidden manna, and I will give him a white stone, with a new name written on the stone which no one knows except him who receives it" (Revelation 2:17 RSV).

8 John Bunyan, *The Pilgrim's Progress* (New York: Simon & Schuster, 1957), 54–55.

9 See, for example, Michael J. Behe, *Darwin's Black Box: The Biochemical Challenge to Evolution* (New York: Free Press, 1996); William A. Dembski, *Intelligent Design: The Bridge Between Science and Theology* (Downers Grove, Ill.: InterVarsity Press, 1999); and the many works of Phillip Johnson.

10 Richard Lewontin, "Billions and Billions of Demons," *The New York Review of Books* (9 January 1997), 31.

11 I have written about these witnesses in several works, although I have sometimes classified and numbered them differently. See J. Budziszewski, *Written on the Heart* (Downers Grove, Ill.: InterVarsity Press, 1997), especially chapter 13; *The Revenge of Conscience* (Dallas: Spence, 1999), especially chapters 2 and 9; and *The Lost World of Moral Law: A Guide for the Persuaded, the Half-Persuaded, and the Wish-I-Were-Persuaded* (Dallas: Spence, 2002), especially chapters 4 and 5.

12 Romans 1:26–27, for example, condemns *disregard* for the witness of sexual design.

Chapter 8.
Issues and Approaches in Working with Internationals

1 Dianne Schmidley and Herman Alvarado, "The Foreign-Born Population in the United States: March 1997 (Update)," Census Bureau, U.S. Department of Commerce (March 1998), available online at http://www.census.gov/population/www/socdemo/foreign.html

2 Bill Mitchell, International Students, Inc., staff in Greensboro, North Carolina; personal correspondence.

3 Insight shared by Bill Mitchell; personal correspondence.

4 Carl Sagan, *Contact* (New York: Pocket Books, 1985), 153.

5 Told by Bill Mitchell; personal correspondence.

6 Bill Mitchell; personal correspondence.

7 Dean Halverson, ed., *The Compact Guide to World Religions* (Minneapolis: Bethany House, 1996), 170.

8 Dick Innes, "The Art of Using Appropriate Vocabulary," in *The Art of Sharing Your Faith,* ed. Joel Heck (Tarrytown, N.Y.: Revell, 1991), 125.

9 Dwight Goddard, ed., *A Buddhist Bible* (Boston: Beacon Press, 1966), 86.

10 Maulana Muhammad Ali, *The Holy Quran* (Chicago: Specialty Promotions, 1985), 918.

11 Halverson, *The Compact Guide to World Religions,* 19–20.

12 Kenny Barfield, *Why the Bible Is Number One* (Grand Rapids: Baker, 1988), 12.

13 William Cairney, "Biomedical Prescience 1: Hebrew Dietary Laws," in *Evidence for Faith: Deciding the God Question,* ed. John Warwick Montgomery (Dallas: Probe Books, 1991), 128.

14 Barfield, *Why the Bible Is Number One,* 102–3.

15 Ibid., 103–6.

16 Ibid., 107.

17 Ibid., 169–70.

18 Ibid., 171–72.

19 See a discussion of how science is supporting the creationist model over the evolutionary model in chapters 6–10, Chuck Colson and Nancy Pearcey, *How Now Shall We Live?* (Wheaton, Ill.: Tyndale House, 1999).

20 Patrick Glynn, *God: The Evidence: The Reconciliation of Faith and Reason in a Postsecular World* (Roseville, Calif.: Prima, 1997), 26.

21 Colson and Pearcey, *How Now Shall We Live?* 57–58.

22 Charles Darwin as quoted in Percival Davis and Dean Kenyon, *Of Pandas and People: The Central Question of Biological Origins,* 2d ed. (Dallas: Haughton, 1993), 23.

23 Colson and Pearcey, *How Now Shall We Live?* 85–86.

24 Ibid., 83.

[25] Ibid., 70.

[26] Michael Behe, *Darwin's Black Box: The Biochemical Challenge to Evolution* (New York: Touchstone, 1996), 172.

[27] Glynn, *God: The Evidence*, 29.

[28] Ibid., 29.

[29] Ibid., 30.

[30] Colson and Pearcey, *How Now Shall We Live?* 62.

[31] Glynn, *God: The Evidence*, 28.

[32] Ibid., 22.

[33] Behe, *Darwin's Black Box*, 39.

[34] Ibid., 39.

[35] Ibid., 204.

[36] Ibid., 39, 73, 194.

[37] Colson and Pearcey, *How Now Shall We Live?* 75.

[38] Ibid., 67.

[39] Paul Copan, *"True for You, but Not for Me": Deflating the Slogans That Leave Christians Speechless* (Minneapolis: Bethany House, 1998), chapter 1.

[40] Ibid., 4.

[41] Ibid., chapter 5.

[42] Ibid., chapter 13.

[43] Ibid., 71.

[44] Ibid., 66.

SCRIPTURE INDEX

Genesis
1:1 136
1:14 136
1:26–27 .... 117, 122
7:11 137
9:6 .... 117, 122

Deuteronomy
6:5–7 .... 90, 91

2 Samuel
22:16 137

Job
26:7 .... 136, 137
38:16 137

Psalms
19 60
19:1–6 122
19:1–4 61
19:12–13 113
36 73
104 122
139:13–14 122

Proverbs
1:31 122
8:28 137
31:26 91

Ecclesiastes
1:2 60

Isaiah
28:23–29 122
40:18 134
40:25 134
55:8–9 .... 109, 134

Jeremiah
17:9 112
17:10 122
31:37 136

Hosea
10:12 122

Zechariah
12:1 136

Matthew
5:11–12 117
5:16 101
7:1 107
19:14 100
26:39 49

Luke
13:1–5 69
16:19–31 20

John
4 83
4:29 .... 83, 96
5:24 68
8:12 47
9:3 69

11:25–26 47
14:6 ....28, 47, 49
20:25 64
20:27 64
20:28 64

Acts
4:12 49
14:17 122
17:22–32 122
17:22–23 80–81
17:23 62
17:24–27 62
17:31 84
19:8–12 56
19:10–11 56
21:8 77

Romans
1:18 122
1:19–20 61
1:20 122
2:15 122
5:6 130
5:8 130
6:23 ....130, 131
8:13 112
8:31 117
8:38–39 133
10:13–15 20
12:2 95

1 Corinthians
2:3–4 81
4:5 117
12:27 108
13 81
13:12 115

Galatians
1:10 117
6:2 108
6:7 122

Ephesians
2:1 130
4:11 77
5:32 111
6 96
6:10–18 118
6:17 78

Philippians
3:20 108
4:8 95

Colossians
3:5 112

1 Thessalonians
2:4 117

1 Timothy
6:16 129

2 Timothy
1:5 91
4:1–5 71
4:5 77

Hebrews
4:12 78
10:25 107
11:1 ....70, 106

James
1:5 98

1 Peter
2:9 108
3:15 ....20, 22, 57, 130
5:7 135

Jude
22 57

Revelation
2:2 84

SUBJECT INDEX

A

abortion, 48–49
apologetics
    and the abortion issue, 48–49
    accessibility of, 92
    atheism and, 29–30
    as attraction, 128–134
    in the church, 56–59
    church as an institution of,
        39–54
    clarifying and defending the
        truth in, 27–28
    classroom, 50–52
    as defense, 135–142
    defining, 21–24, 39–40, 101
    divisiveness of, 91
    and doubt in unbelievers,
        62–66
    and Eastern mysticism,
        45–46
    and evolution, 51, 137–142
    existential persuasion and,
        40–42
    gospel on, 22–24, 55–56
    and Jesus as more than a
        great religious leader,
        46–48
    minimization of, 55–56
    misconceptions about, 91–94
    as offense, 142–146

    pastors and, 21–30
    in preaching, 44–50, 49–50,
        70–71
    and the purpose and mean-
        ing of life, 59–62
    relevance of, 93–94
    removing the obstacles to
        truth, 28–30
    and responding to bad times,
        67–70
    strategies for the church,
        52–53
    teaching children, 99–101
    worship and, 42–44
atheism, 26, 29–30
attraction, apologetics as,
    128–134

B

Barclay, William, 81
Barfield, Kenny, 136
Barnhouse, Donald Grey, 92
Behe, Michael, 51, 140–141
Bible, the, 61–62, 136–137.
    See also gospel, the
Bloom, Allan, 45
Boreham, F. W., 18–19
Buddhism, 23, 27, 128, 130–131,
    134, 146
Bunyan, John, 96, 119

C

Cairney, William, 136
Case for Christ, The, 51, 100
children
and the media, 94–96
passing the torch to, 89–91
teaching opportunities for,
96–98
training parents to teach,
99–101
Chronicles of Narnia, The, 96
*Closing of the American Mind,
The,* 45
coherence of truth statements,
27–28
college students
calling bluffs, 121–122
and colleges at war with
Christianity, 103–104
and the desires and devices
of their hearts, 112–113
and the faith commitments
of their adversaries,
119–121
and the limits of good intentions, 113–114
and moral judgment, 106,
116–117
necessary preparation for,
107–122
reasons for losing faith,
104–107
and the relations between
faith and knowledge,
115–116
resisting nonbelievers,
117–119
and revelation, 105, 109–110
sentimentalism in, 114–115
and sexuality, 104–106,
110–112, 113–114

congregational life, 41–42, 43,
99–101
Copan, Paul, 144
Crabb, Larry, 69

D

Darwin, Charles, 138, 140
Darwin on Trial, 51
Darwin's Black Box, 51, 140
death, 18–19, 67–68
De Chardin, Teilhard, 67

E

Eastern mysticism, 45–46
Einstein, Albert, 136
Ellul, Jacques, 19
emotions
approaching internationals
through their, 133–134
effect on truth, 32–33,
114–115
faith and, 36–37
pastors bringing balance
between mind and,
35–37
evangelism
basic approach to, 82–84
defining, 77–78
identification and, 82–83
justification and, 84
music as, 84–85
persuasion and, 84
preaching as, 78–80, 87
translation and, 83–84
worship as, 85–87
*Evidence for Faith: Deciding
the God Question,* 136
evolution, theory of, 51,
137–142
existential persuasion, 40–42

F

faith, 36–37
  and apologetics, 40–42
  during bad times, 67–70
  commitments of unbeliev-
    ers, 119–121
  defending one's, 117–119
  and doubt in unbelievers,
    62–66
  fellowship of, 44
  reasons college Christians
    lose, 104–107
  relation to knowledge,
    115–116
funerals, 18–19

G

Geisler, Norman, 92
general revelation, 122
gentleness and respect, 37
Glynn, Patrick, 140
God
  internationals attitudes
    toward, 128–130, 145
  as a personal being, 134–135
gospel, the
  apologetics and, 22–24,
    55–56
  defending, 33–35, 135–142
  distortion of, 75–76
  faith and, 36–37
  framing, 15–18
  giving specific answers by
    considering the ques-
    tioner's worldview,
    30–35
  good news/bad news in,
    130–133
  Jesus Christ as the heart of,
    76–77

obstacles to the impact of,
    25, 28–30, 67–70
  preaching, 19–20
  questioning the relevance of,
    75–76
  and the reasonableness of
    revelation, 105,
    109–110
  science in, 61–62, 136–137
  truth of, 15–19, 26–28, 49
Gould, Stephen Jay, 138
Graham, Billy, 43
Guinness, Os, 25, 26, 28, 63

H

Habermas, Gary, 62–63
Hinduism, 27, 127, 128, 130, 146
Holy Spirit, 56–57

I

identification with listeners
  mind-sets, 82–83
information overload, 20–22
intentions, limits of good,
    113–114
internationals
  apologetics as defense
    against, 135–142
  apologetics as offense
    toward, 142–146
  approached through emo-
    tions and imagination,
    133–134
  attitudes toward God,
    128–130, 134–135, 145
  building friendships with,
    126–127, 147

demonstrating hope to, 130
diversity and numbers of,
125–126
and the science of the Bible,
136–137
and the theory of evolution,
137–142
using the good news/bad
news principle with,
130–133
working with, 146
In Two Minds, 63

J

Jesus Christ
framing the gospel of, 15–18
as just one of the world's
great religious leaders,
46–48
on moral judgment, 106,
116–117
power of, 76–77
and the purpose and mean-
ing of life, 61
and the story of Lazarus and
the rich man, 20
and Thomas's doubt, 63–65
on tragedy and suffering, 69
as the truth, 28, 35
as the way to heaven, 49–50
Johnson, Phillip, 51
justification, 84

K

Kreeft, Peter, 31

L

Lazarus and the rich man, 20

leaders, church
apologetics and, 70–71
as apologists, 21–24, 55–56
attending funerals, 18–19
bringing balance between
heart and mind, 35–37
clarifying truth claims,
26–28
communicating with college
students, 107–122
considering questioners'
worldviews, 30–35
defending the truth, 27–28
as evangelists, 77–84
gentleness and respect by, 37
information overload on,
20–22
preaching by, 19–20
removing obstacles to the
gospel, 28–30
roles of, 18–19
using the three levels of philosophy, 31–35
Lewis, C. S., 46–47, 51–52, 60,
64, 65, 70, 74, 96
Lewontin, Richard, 120
logic, 31–32

M

Luther, Martin, 78–79
marriage, 66
Martin, Walter, 100
McDowell, Dottie, 99
McDowell, Josh, 52, 92, 99
media, the, 94–96
Mere Christianity, 46–47, 52, 64,
65
Miller, Dale, 100
Miller, Stanley, 139

misconceptions about
apologetics, 91–94
Mitchell, Bill, 130
moral judgment, 106, 116–117
Moreland, J. P., 92, 101
More Than a Carpenter, 52
Morgenthaler, Sally, 42
Moses, 20
Muggeridge, Malcolm, 76
music as evangelism, 84–85
Muslims, 127, 128, 131,
134–135, 145, 146
My God Is Real, 65

N

*New Evidence That Demands a
Verdict*, 92

O

Origen, 73–74, 76–77, 78
Origin of Species, The, 138

P

parents
and the media, 94–96
passing the torch, 89–91
teaching opportunities for,
96–98
training for, 99–101
pastors. *See* leaders, church
Paul, the apostle, 80–82, 88
Peacocke, Arthur, 75
persuasion, 84
Petersen, Jim, 57–58
philosophy, three levels of,
31–35
Pilgrim's Progress, The, 96, 119
postmodernism, 119–121

prayer, 50, 86–87, 87, 114, 146
preaching, 19–20, 73–74
apologetics in, 44–50, 49–50,
70–71
in casual conversations, 33
as evangelism, 78–80, 87
to skeptics, 80–82
proclamation, 82–84
Promise Keepers, 43

R

racial discrimination, 34
reality
emotions and, 32–33
logic and, 31–32
and three levels of philosophy, 31–35
truth and, 27–28
reasonableness of revelation,
109–110
reincarnation, 45–46, 144
relativism, 45, 48
revelation, 105, 109–110
Rousseau, Jean-Jacques, 58

S

Sagan, Carl, 128–129
Sayers, Dorothy, 44–45, 54
Scaling the Secular City, 92
Schaeffer, Francis, 26
science of the Bible, 61–62,
136–142
Screwtape Letters, The, 74
sexuality, 30, 34–35
and college Christians,
104–106, 110–112,
113–114
skepticism, 15, 43, 51, 58, 80–82
Smith, Gypsy, 22

Stott, John, 23
Strobel, Lee, 51
subjectivism, 45, 48

T

teaching apologetics, 50–52
Temple, William, 85–86
Three Philosophies of Life, 31
Topsy-Turvy Kingdom, The, 99
Tozer, A. W., 23–24
translation, 83–84
truth
　about life's purpose and
　　meaning, 59–62
　and the balance between
　　heart and mind, 35–37
　clarifying claims of, 26–28
　coherence of, 27–28
　correspondence to reality
　　of, 27–28
　defending, 27–28
　emotions' effect on, 32–33,
　　114–115
　removing obstacles to,
　　28–30
　skepticism and, 15, 43, 51,
　　58, 80–82
　television and, 16
　and the Western way of
　　thinking, 27

U

unbelievers
　apologetics for reaching,
　　58–59
　calling bluffs of, 121–122
　faith and doubt in, 62–66
　faith commitments of,
　　119–121
　and postmodernism,
　　119–121
　preaching to, 80–82
　questions about life's pur-
　　pose and meaning,
　　59–62
　reactions to bad times,
　　67–70
　resisting, 117–119

W

Watson, David, 65
What Dreams May Come,
　133–134
When Skeptics Ask, 92
Why the Bible Is Number One,
　136
worship
　and apologetics, 42–44
　as evangelism, 85–87
Worship Evangelism, 42

WHO MADE GOD?

AND ANSWERS TO OVER 100 OTHER TOUGH QUESTIONS OF FAITH

RAVI ZACHARIAS
NORMAN GEISLER

GENERAL EDITORS

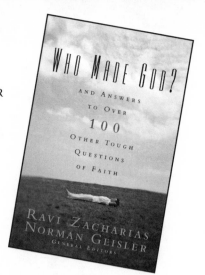

Answers to the Most-Asked Questions about the Christian Faith

In the quest for the truth, you need to know what you believe and why you believe it. *Who Made God?* offers accessible answers to over 100 commonly asked apologetic questions. Bringing together the best in evangelical apologists, this guide is standard equipment for Christians who want to understand and intelligently talk about their faith.

Part 1 answers tough questions about the Christian faith such as:
- Who made God?
- How can there be three persons in one God?
- What is God's ultimate purpose in allowing evil?
- Wouldn't it be better if God did away with all evil immediately?
- Where did the universe come from?
- How long are the days of creation in Genesis?
- Did Jesus rise from the dead?
- Are the records of Jesus' life reliable?
- Does the Bible have errors in it?
- Could prophets add their personal thoughts to God's message?

Part 2 answers tough questions about other faiths, including Islam, Mormonism, Hinduism, Transcendental Meditation, Yoga, Reincarnation, Buddhism, and Black Islam. Relevant stories, questions for reflection and discussion, and a comprehensive list of suggested resources help you dig deeper so you can be prepared to give careful answers that explain the reasons for your faith.

Softcover ISBN 0-310-24710-1

Pick up a copy at your favorite bookstore!

GRAND RAPIDS, MICHIGAN 49530 USA

WWW.ZONDERVAN.COM

We want to hear from you. Please send your comments about this book to us in care of zreview@zondervan.com. Thank you.

GRAND RAPIDS, MICHIGAN 49530 USA

WWW.ZONDERVAN.COM